LOVE AND UNDERSTANDING

BY JOE PENHALL

DRAMATISTS
PLAY SERVICE
INC.

LOVE AND UNDERSTANDING
Copyright © 1999, Joe Penhall
ALL RIGHTS RESERVED

CAUTION: Professionals and amateurs are hereby warned that performance of LOVE AND UNDERSTANDING is subject to a royalty. It is fully protected under the copyright laws of the United States of America, and of all countries covered by the International Copyright Union (including the Dominion of Canada and the rest of the British Commonwealth), and of all countries covered by the Pan-American Copyright Convention and the Universal Copyright Convention, the Berne Convention, and of all countries with which the United States has reciprocal copyright relations. All rights, including professional/amateur stage rights, motion picture, recitation, lecturing, public reading, radio broadcasting, television, video or sound recording, all other forms of mechanical or electronic reproduction, such as CD-ROM, CD-I, DVD, information storage and retrieval systems and photocopying, and the rights of translation into foreign languages, are strictly reserved. Particular emphasis is placed upon the question of readings, permission for which must be secured from the Author's agent in writing.

The English language stage performance rights in the United States, its territories and possessions and the Dominion of Canada for LOVE AND UNDERSTANDING are controlled exclusively by the DRAMATISTS PLAY SERVICE, INC., 440 Park Avenue South, New York, N.Y. 10016. No professional or non-professional performance of the Play may be given without obtaining in advance the written permission of the DRAMATISTS PLAY SERVICE, INC., and paying the requisite fee.

Inquiries concerning all other rights in the United States and Canada should be addressed to William Morris Agency, Inc., 1325 Avenue of the Americas, New York, NY 10019, Attn: Gilbert Parker; and rights elsewhere to ICM, Oxford House, 76 Oxford Street, London W1N OAX, Attn: Alan Radcliffe.

SPECIAL NOTE

Anyone receiving permission to produce LOVE AND UNDERSTANDING is required to (1) give credit to the Author as sole and exclusive Author of the Play on the title page of all programs distributed in connection with performances of the Play and in all instances in which the title of the Play appears for purposes of advertising, publicizing or otherwise exploiting the Play and/or a production thereof. The name of the Author must appear on a separate line, in which no other name appears, immediately beneath the title and in size of type equal to 50% of the size of the largest most prominent letter used for the title of the Play. No person, firm or entity may receive credit larger or more prominent that that accorded the Author; and (2) to give the following acknowledgment on the title page in all programs distribute in connection with performances of the Play:

LOVE AND UNDERSTANDING was initially produced by the Bush Theatre, London, England

| Mike Bradwell | Deborah Aydon |
| Artistic Director | General Manager |

April 30, 1997

American Premiere production presented at the Long Wharf Theatre

| Douglas Hughes | Michael Ross |
| Artistic Director | Managing Director |

March 13, 1998

Original music composed by Joe Penhall, Brian Penhall and Caleb Faucett

LOVE AND UNDERSTANDING received its premiere at the Bush Theatre (Michael Bradwell, Artistic Director) in London, England, on April 30, 1997. It was directed by Mike Bradwell; the design was by Es Devlin; the lighting design was by Kevin Sleep; the sound design was by Simon Whitehorn; the original music was by Joe Penhall, Brian Penhall and Caleb Fawcett; and the stage managers were Rob Bishop, Zoë Grant, and Katherine Mahoney. The cast was as follows:

RICHIE .... Paul Bettany
RACHEL .... Celia Robertson
NEAL .... Nicolas Tennant

LOVE AND UNDERSTANDING was produced by Long Wharf Theatre (Doug Hughes, Artistic Director) and the Bush Theatre (Michael Bradwell, Artistic Director) in New Haven, Connecticut, on March 13, 1998. It was directed by Mike Bradwell; the set and costume designs were by Es Devlin; the lighting design was by Rick Fisher; the sound design was by Simon Whitehorn; and the production stage manager was Daniel S. Rosokoff. The cast was as follows:

RICHIE ....Paul Bettany
RACHEL ....Celia Robertson
NEAL ....Nicolas Tennant

LOVE AND UNDERSTANDING

ACT ONE

Scene 1

Neal and Rachel's flat. Early Morning. Neal and Richie standing in the kitchen. Richie drinking a pint of milk, a suitcase at his feet. A plane is heard overhead.

NEAL. We're under the flight path. One every two minutes.
RICHIE. Very nice. All yours?
NEAL. Will be one day.
RICHIE. I'm impressed.
NEAL. It actually works out a lot cheaper than renting.
RICHIE. Well, that's the clincher isn't it?
NEAL. It's got a good bathroom.
RICHIE. A bathroom and everything? Wow. Have you got a shower?
NEAL. Got a very nice shower.
RICHIE. A very nice shower? Well, that's very nice isn't it? *(He looks around, takes a few steps.)* Very clean. *(Pause.)*
NEAL. How's Nicky?
RICHIE. Who?
NEAL. Nicky. Your girlfriend. *(Pause.)*
RICHIE. Oh. We split up.
NEAL. Again?
RICHIE. It's for real this time.

NEAL. That's what you said last time.
RICHIE. It's for real this time.
NEAL. Well ... why?
RICHIE. I hit her.
NEAL. You hit her?
RICHIE. That's when it started to get ugly.
NEAL. Jesus ...
RICHIE. That's what she said.
NEAL. My God. That's terrible. *(Pause.)* Then what happened?
RICHIE. Then she hit me.
NEAL. I don't believe it.
RICHIE. That's what I said.
NEAL. You must have really provoked her.
RICHIE. I suppose I must have. *(Pause.)*
NEAL. How hard did you hit her?
RICHIE. Not very hard. Hard enough to give her a black eye but that's only because she has very delicate skin. *(Pause.)* The point is Nicky is absolutely the wrong person to hit. She hates violence. She even hates shouting.
NEAL. Well, I know ...
RICHIE. I mean it really pissed her off. That kind of thing really freaks her out.
NEAL. It freaks me out.
RICHIE. It freaks me out. I've never been so freaked in my life. *(Pause.)*
NEAL. But you were so in love.
RICHIE. I loved her to bits. It was love at first.
NEAL. I remember you telling me.
RICHIE. It was the real thing.
NEAL. What went wrong?
RICHIE. Well that's just it. Who knows? One minute things were fine and the next minute ... wham.
NEAL. It's ridiculous.
RICHIE. It's absurd. *(Pause.)*
NEAL. So where is she now?
RICHIE. I haven't the faintest idea. Somewhere in South America.
NEAL. Oh my God. When's she coming home?

RICHIE. She could be home tomorrow or in two years time. She's like that. She's a very impulsive woman. *(Pause.)*
NEAL. Well, you like impulsive women.
RICHIE. Impulsive women are great.
NEAL. Depending on the impulse.
RICHIE. Oh, it depends entirely on the impulse. *(Pause.)* How's Rachel?
NEAL. Fine.
RICHIE. Happy?
NEAL. How d'you mean?
RICHIE. Is she happy? You know, as opposed to sad.
NEAL. I think she's happy. She spent most of this week sleeping.
RICHIE. Perhaps she was sleepy.
NEAL. Actually she's not all that well at the moment. She's just finished six months on a children's ward so she's full of bugs and sniffles.
RICHIE. Poor thing. Can't you do anything for her?
NEAL. Well ... it goes with the territory.
RICHIE. But you're a doctor. You're both doctors. It doesn't seem very fair.
NEAL. Well it isn't. Absolutely. Still ... *(Pause.)*
RICHIE. Are you ready to tie the knot yet?
NEAL. No nothing like that.
RICHIE. Why not?
NEAL. We're happy as we are.
RICHIE. I'd marry Nicky tomorrow if ... she didn't hate me ...
NEAL. Well ... to be honest I don't think Rachel's really the marrying type. She likes her independence.
RICHIE. Really? She never struck me as the independent type.
NEAL. She's not the marrying type, that's all I know.
RICHIE. Really? I'm surprised. *(Pause.)* Have you asked her?
NEAL. Good God no.
RICHIE. Why not?
NEAL. I just don't think she's ready.
RICHIE. Well the day you get spliced I'm your best man, all right?
NEAL. Well, you never know ...
RICHIE. Well absolutely. You do never know. Until you ask her.

NEAL. Oh of course ...
RICHIE. I mean it. I'd get a big bang out of that.
NEAL. Of course ... *(Richie straightens Neal's tie. Pause.)* So, where else have you been?
RICHIE. In Boston. Writing for *The Globe*.
NEAL. The Boston *Globe*?
RICHIE. Fenway Park *Globe*. The Boston Redsox were having a good year and they needed every hack they could lay their hands on. They hadn't won a series since 1920 when they sold Babe Ruth to the Yankees. They call it The Curse. Not long after I arrived they started losing again.
NEAL. The last time I saw you you were chasing ambulances and interviewing models from Croydon who used to work in a bakery.
RICHIE. Funny isn't it?
NEAL. Incredible ... You got any copies?
RICHIE. How do you mean?
NEAL. The stories for *The Globe*.
RICHIE. I never show my work before it's published. It lets the air out of the tyres. *(Pause.)*
NEAL. It's not published?
RICHIE. No. Should it be?
NEAL. Well ... yes.
RICHIE. Listen. I've just flown six thousand miles. Any danger of a cup of tea?
NEAL. Coffee.
RICHIE. Is it fresh? I only drink fresh coffee now. Ever since Ecuador. *(Neal prepares coffee. Richie takes out a packet of cigarettes and lights one, coughs. Sips milk.)*
NEAL. Oh. I'd rather you didn't do that in here ...
RICHIE. Why not?
NEAL. My clothes will smell of smoke. It's not very pleasant for my patients.
RICHIE. So?
NEAL. Well ... do you mind going outside?
RICHIE. You really want me to go outside?
NEAL. If that's OK ...
RICHIE. It's a bit chilly ...

NEAL. I don't think so ... We're in the middle of a heat wave.
RICHIE. You call this a heat wave?
NEAL. Well, I don't smoke and nor does Rachel. It really wouldn't be fair.
RICHIE. I'll lose my train of thought. I might lose my entire inclination. Do you really think that's fair, Neal? *(Neal puts an ashtray down.)* I'll get lonely.
NEAL. How would you like your coffee?
RICHIE. Answer my question. Is it, or isn't it fair?
NEAL. How do you have your coffee?
RICHIE. It isn't fair. It's unfair, isn't it? Cream with about six sugars. *(Neal takes the milk from Richie, prepares coffee. Richie opens his case and hands a bottle of Scotch to Neal.)* Put a drop of that in will you? *(Neal pours, hands Richie the coffee. Richie takes the Scotch and adds more.)*
NEAL. Have you seen your dad yet? *(Pause.)* Richie?
RICHIE. No. Why?
NEAL. I just thought you could go and stay with him.
RICHIE. Oh I see ... well ... I'd rather stay here.
NEAL. Well the thing is ...
RICHIE. What? *(Richie pours more whisky into his coffee. Sips.)*
NEAL. Did you ring your mum to say you were back?
RICHIE. Of course I did.
NEAL. What did she say?
RICHIE. She said, "Oh, that's nice." Anyway, I didn't come all this way to see them, I came all this way to see you and Rachel. No ... I'd much rather stay here. *(Pause.)*
NEAL. You have a very strange relationship with your parents, don't you Richie?
RICHIE. I have a very strange relationship with everybody, Neal. If you don't know that by now you soon will. *(Pause.)*
NEAL. Well ... how long were you planning on staying?
RICHIE. How long can I stay?
NEAL. I'll have to talk to Rachel.
RICHIE. I'll talk to her.
NEAL. I'll talk to her, Rich.
RICHIE. OK. But don't take any shit.
NEAL. How do you mean?

RICHIE. Don't let her manipulate you.
NEAL. Manipulate me? What on earth makes you think she'll do that?
RICHIE. Well, I expect she's quite stern about this sort of thing.
NEAL. What do you mean, "stern"?
RICHIE. Well, I'm sure she has her rules.
NEAL. We just have to agree. Nothing to do with being stern.
RICHIE. Oh, I like stern women. Stern women are great. *(Neal produces a blanket and pillow and puts them on the sofa.)*
NEAL. I should get to work.
RICHIE. I wouldn't mind a kip now. Shake off some of that jet lag.
NEAL. Well ... feel free to use the sofa.
RICHIE. Haven't you got a bed?
NEAL. I just told you. Rachel's asleep.
RICHIE. Can't you wake her up? I'm shagged.
NEAL. She's been working very hard.
RICHIE. Neal ... I'm winding you up. I'll be fine. *(Richie goes to the sofa, takes the blanket and wraps it around himself. He sits on the sofa with his feet up and drinks from the whisky bottle.)* Safe as milk. *(Richie drinks.)* Sound as a pound.
NEAL. I think it's a little early to be ...
RICHIE. I'm thirsty. You have no idea how those jumbos dehydrate you. *(Neal picks up his case and jacket and goes to the door. Richie suddenly winces.)* Fuck.
NEAL. Are you all right?
RICHIE. Just a bit of a headache. Just ... severe stabbing pains in my head. I've had them for months. Probably all the flying ...
NEAL. You should get out in the fresh air, clear your lungs, take your mind off things.
RICHIE. Are you trying to get me out of the house?
NEAL. No of course not ... *(Pause.)* Of course not ... I just don't want any ...
RICHIE. Any what, Neal? Wild parties? I came here because I thought you'd understand.
NEAL. I do.
RICHIE. Maybe you could fix me up with something. Pain killers. I am really in quite a lot of pain. *(Richie drinks.)*

NEAL. Well ... if it's serious you should come to the hospital. Have a scan.
RICHIE. Come to the hospital? Now?
NEAL. When you've rested.
RICHIE. I'd love to come to the hospital. I've been waiting for you to invite me.
NEAL. When you've rested.
RICHIE. I'm rested now.
NEAL. Actually, Richie. I've got a very busy morning.
RICHIE. I don't mind.
NEAL. No. I'm really snowed under at the moment.
RICHIE. I don't mind.

Scene 2

Hospital. Morning. Neal sitting at a desk looking at scans. Richie, shirtless, sitting in a chair.

RICHIE. I've always liked Rachel. Nice, uncomplicated ... clean. I bet she wears Marks and Spencers underwear, am I right?
NEAL. Actually, sometimes she doesn't wear any underwear.
RICHIE. No. No knickers? It's always the quiet ones. *(Neal produces a* Gray's Anatomy *and tries to read.)* When my relationship with Nicky went West I vowed that the next relationship I had would be with somebody rather bourgeois and conventional. Dull even. A woman who doesn't crave alcohol or drugs, isn't particularly promiscuous, not remotely interested in danger and machismo ... finds daytime TV entertaining and informative. No spiritual life whatsoever ... you know the sort. They're less flighty and sometimes, I suspect, more sincere.
NEAL. Really?
RICHIE. Really. Where do I get a woman like that?
NEAL. You just keep your hands to yourself ...

RICHIE.   I bet you two have fun playing doctors and nurses. Or is doctors and doctors better? You could have a ball. Rubber gloves. Stirrups. Outrageous. *(Neal sighs and goes back to his writing.)* I love the smell of hospitals. The cleaning fluids, the raw alcohol, the ethanol, the pervasive air of a thousand highly expensive intravenous drugs doing their benevolent task. The nurses mincing about in their crisp, clean, starched uniforms. I adore nurses ... You know, places like this really bring out the Anglo-Saxon in me. Have you got any milk? *(Richie opens the fridge.)*
NEAL.   Stay out of that will you?
RICHIE.   I'm looking for milk.
NEAL.   The only milk you'll find in there is milk of magnesia. *(Richie takes a vial from the fridge and examines it.)*
RICHIE.   You know, you could make a fortune out of this.
NEAL.   Richie please. You're making me nervous ... *(Richie shuts the fridge and sits down. Pause.)* I can't see anything wrong with you. You're fine. *(Richie rests his head on the desk.)* Richie?
RICHIE.   How about a shot of morphine? That'll perk me up.
NEAL.   Morphine? No ...
RICHIE.   Oh come on ...
NEAL.   What do you want morphine for?
RICHIE.   You mean you've never tried it? But you're a doctor.
NEAL.   Are you some kind of junkie now?
RICHIE.   A what? A "junkie"? *(Richie laughs.)* Well, strictly speaking, I'm a speed freak. *(Pause.)* No but seriously ... it's a form of self-medication. *(Pause.)* I get ... depressed.
NEAL.   I'm not surprised.
RICHIE.   Do you think it's funny?
NEAL.   No. Do you really get depressed? Real depression?
RICHIE.   Well, overwhelming melancholy, certainly. Give me a shot of morphine and I'll leave you alone. *(Pause.)*
NEAL.   No. I'm sorry.
RICHIE.   Come on. Don't be such a spoilsport.
NEAL.   Look ... at the end of the day all these drugs do is induce a state of euphoria no greater or less than you'd get from eating a good steak, having a roll in the hay with your girlfriend

or going to bed early with a good book for that matter. It's a waste of time.

RICHIE.   I don't have a girlfriend anymore. *(Pause.)*

NEAL.   The thing is Richie, you've come at a bit of a bad time.

RICHIE.   Tell me your problems then. Come on. Talk to me. I'm listening. *(Pause.)*

NEAL.   I've got too much responsibility. I'm in charge of intensive care and I shouldn't be. I'm working every day and every night. I never see Rachel because she's working every day and every night. We haven't talked properly in three weeks. We communicate by post-it notes. Answerphone messages, for God's sake.

RICHIE.   I hate those things.

NEAL.   So do I. But what else can we do?

RICHIE.   I hate those ones with the tunes. You know those tacky fucking tunes?

NEAL.   So do I. So I leave a note saying, Let's go out to dinner. Let's set aside a time for each other. Then she leaves a note saying, Yes, good idea. Only I don't get the note, because it's taken me a few days to find it and she's tidied it up, in a hurry to get to work. I don't know this, so after a few days I leave a message on the answerphone saying, Do you want to go out to dinner or not? And she leaves one saying, Of course, I already said I did. So I leave another note saying, You didn't actually but anyway, when? Then she leaves a note saying, I damn well did and I don't really like the tone of your message. Now there's something in my tone that she doesn't like ... or something in her tone that I don't like ... and on it goes. On and on and on. I don't know what to do. I'm at my wit's end. I mean it really is a dilemma. *(Pause.)*

RICHIE.   Have you tried paging her?

NEAL.   I mean it Rich. Things have been a bit funny with us lately.

RICHIE.   Funny ha ha or funny strange?

NEAL.   Are you listening to me? *(Pause.)*

RICHIE.   Are you still sleeping together?

NEAL.   How do you mean?

RICHIE. I mean what about bedtime? Talk to her at bedtime.
NEAL. We're asleep by bedtime. I stagger in, shagged, fall asleep. She staggers in shagged, falls asleep, one of us wakes up and the other's gone to work ... there's just no ... there just doesn't seem to be any ...
RICHIE. Shagging?
NEAL. Chance would be a fine thing ...
RICHIE. None at all?
NEAL. Not lately, no ...
RICHIE. How lately?
NEAL. Does it matter?
RICHIE. Well ... yes ...
NEAL. I don't really want to go into it ...
RICHIE. Well of course you don't. No, of course not. I mean it's none of my business, obviously. *(Pause.)* I just find it astounding. *(Pause.)* I find it astonishing ... no sex ...
NEAL. Richie ...
RICHIE. I'm staggered. I don't know what to say ...
NEAL. Richie!
RICHIE. You really are in a state aren't you?
NEAL. I just have a few things to sort out that's all. A few things on my mind.
RICHIE. It's not me is it? I'm not getting on your nerves am I? Because you know me. If I can help in any way you only have to say. Can I borrow some money?
NEAL. Look, I'm trying to tell you ... I'm just saying ... we need some time to ourselves.
RICHIE. And I'm just saying, relax. I'm here now. You and me are going to have a good time. *(Richie punches Neal's arm playfully. Neal just looks at him.)* So can I borrow some money or what?
NEAL. How much do you want?
RICHIE. How much have you got? *(Neal takes out his wallet.)* I've got a fifty and a tenner.
RICHIE. Well a tenner's not going to get me very far is it?
NEAL. It's all I have. *(He hands Richie the tenner.)*
RICHIE. You must have more.
NEAL. I don't.
RICHIE. Give me the fifty and I'll buy you a drink tonight.

NEAL. I'm busy tonight.
RICHIE. Have a night off. One night off Neal. One night with your lovely girlfriend and your old pal. Marvelous. *(Pause.)*
NEAL. Actually, I'm taking Rachel out to dinner tonight.
RICHIE. Oh. So you're not working tonight.
NEAL. No.
RICHIE. Oh. I see. That was all a lie, was it?
NEAL. I just want to get her on her own for a few hours and ... you know ...
RICHIE. Fuck her brains out. Absolutely ...
NEAL. Make contact. It's important to me Rich. *(Pause.)*
RICHIE. Anywhere in mind?
NEAL. There's a nice French restaurant in the Fulham Road. By the police station.
RICHIE. It's a dump. I reviewed it once. The lamb's like dog food.
NEAL. Well we'll have a curry then ...
RICHIE. No, I can't have a curry now. I need English food.
NEAL. You're not coming.
RICHIE. What's wrong with the pub? That'll loosen her up.
NEAL. Do you understand?
RICHIE. Absolutely. I understand. I'm not completely insensitive.

Scene 3

Pub. Evening. Richie, Neal and Rachel sitting at a garden table.

RICHIE. After Patzcuaro, we traveled around for a bit and went to Oaxaca, which is like a trendy student town, a sort of mixture of Acapulco and Bristol, really. Lots of wrought iron and vegetarian tortilla houses. Then we got a boat across the lake to San Pedro. Volcano town. A great blue fire-breathing plutonic

rock placed in a bright green wilderness by God himself. Beautiful. I mean, really spectacular, Neal. We were in paradise. A nice hotel room with a balcony overlooking the water, pissed every night on tequila, everything in its rightful place. We were very content Neal. Astonishingly happy ...
NEAL. We went to Richmond once. Went rowing in a rowing boat. On the river. You can hire them for a fiver. Lots of people do it ...
RICHIE. Sometime around Christmas a man called Carlos moved into the next room. We got to know him on New Year's eve when Nicky invited him in for a drink. My God, what a character ... *"Yo hablo buenas historias!"* he said. "I speak the good story!" And by fuck did he have some stories ...
NEAL. My God, is that the time? Is anybody hungry?
RICHIE. I could murder another Scotch.
NEAL. I'm hungry. Are you hungry?
RACHEL. Yes. Let's eat.
RICHIE. But we've only just got here. Have another drink. Work up an appetite.
NEAL. No I think we'll get going now. I booked the table for eight.
RICHIE. Have another drink.
NEAL. It's half past now.
RICHIE. You'll be fashionably late.
RACHEL. I don't want another drink.
NEAL. I don't want another drink either.
RICHIE. I'll tell you what. I'll get the round in while you make up your minds. *(Richie goes. Pause.)*
NEAL. Well. This is nice, isn't it?
RACHEL. Oh, I don't mind.
NEAL. I do. We're meant to be going out to dinner.
RACHEL. Well, tell him.
NEAL. I've told him. I made it absolutely clear.
RACHEL. What did he say?
NEAL. He doesn't care. *(Pause.)*
RACHEL. Well. I don't suppose it matters.
NEAL. It bloody well does.

RACHEL. Neal, don't snap at me.
NEAL. I'm sorry.
RACHEL. Well, what's upsetting you?
NEAL. Him.
RACHEL. Why?
NEAL. I can't explain it. I'm just on a short fuse at the moment.
RACHEL. Look. We'll have a nice drink, he can finish all his silly stories and then we can find him a hotel. All right? *(Pause.)*
NEAL. I've been meaning to talk to you about that.
RACHEL. Why?
NEAL. ... I think he wants to stay for a few days.
RACHEL. Well he can't.
NEAL. I know. That's what I said.
RACHEL. Well he can, but we're both working. I don't know what he's going to do with himself.
NEAL. I know. That's what I said.
RACHEL. And what did he say?
NEAL. He doesn't care. *(Pause.)*
RACHEL. I'll talk to him.
NEAL. You can try.
RACHEL. I will
NEAL. But don't let him manipulate you.
RACHEL. What do you mean?
NEAL. You know what he's like.
RACHEL. Oh, he's just a bit of a chancer. He'll get the message. *(Richie returns with white powder around his nose. He places the drinks and sits rubbing his nose and sniffing, grinding his teeth and so forth. Neal looks at him and indicates, Richie just stares.)*
RICHIE. ... So meanwhile, the main coke dealer in town was a former CIA agent riddled with nine types of cancer.
NEAL. Richie ... *(Neal indicates again.)*
RICHIE. Oh ... thanks ... *(Richie wipes his nose.)* He called himself Jack but his real name was Simon. I don't know, that's the CIA for you. They pride themselves simultaneously on their lively intellect and their macho Celtic roots ...
NEAL. The CIA?
RICHIE. Something like that, yes. Does it matter?

NEAL. Well ... yes.
RICHIE. All right. He was a piano tuner from Scunthorpe who'd just won the lottery. He was a plumber from Nebraska ... do you want to hear this story or not?
NEAL. ... No ...
RICHIE. Personally, I couldn't bare the cunt but Nicky developed a strong affection for him.
NEAL. Richie, please ...
RICHIE. I spent a lot of time drunk. They spent a lot of time together. There was a chemistry between them and I was ... nervous but at the same time ... strangely excited.
RACHEL. You don't have to tell us this. It's none of our business ...
NEAL. Absolutely. None of our business. Drink up ...
RICHIE. She was the first person in a decade who'd listened to his bullshit without looking at her watch.
NEAL. Mm-hm. You're blaming the break up of your relationship on the CIA? *(Neal laughs and stands.)* Is it just me, or is that the funniest fucking thing you've ever heard in your entire life? *(Neal starts to go.)*
RICHIE. Are you done?
NEAL. Sorry?
RICHIE. Have you finished?
NEAL. I was only saying ...
RICHIE. What? What exactly are you saying Neal? *(Neal sits. Pause.)* It wasn't sexual. No doubt about that. I checked.
NEAL. How did you check?
RICHIE. I asked her.
NEAL. You asked her? Priceless ...
RICHIE. Why do you think I'm here?
NEAL. You really asked her that?
RACHEL. Shut up Neal ...
RICHIE. Yes, Neal. I asked her. And it haunts me to this day that such a delightful relationship could be ruined by something so tragically ridiculous but ... *c'est la vie. (Pause.)*
NEAL. When are you going to stop telling these absurd stories? It's like an evening with Graham Greene. I don't think even you can tell when you're lying anymore.

RICHIE. Are you calling me a liar?
NEAL. Yes. I wasn't being subtle.
RICHIE. What do you mean, "a liar"? *(Silence.)*
NEAL. I'll call the restaurant. Tell them we're on our way. *(Neal goes. Silence.)*
RACHEL. So. Have you found somewhere to stay?
RICHIE. How do you mean?
RACHEL. Have you found a hotel?
RICHIE. Well ... I'm staying with you, aren't I?
RACHEL. Oh. Really?
RICHIE. Well ... I mean if that's all right. *(Pause.)* Didn't Neal talk to you about it?
RACHEL. Oh, he mentioned something ...
RICHIE. He said he was going to talk to you about it. I mean ... he said you were going through a bit of a rough patch and ... I mean I understand if it's a problem.
RACHEL. Well, we're just very busy at the moment ...
RICHIE. Absolutely. I mean, he said you were pretty ... stern about this sort of thing. I mean, he did warn me ...
RACHEL. "Stern"? What do you mean, "warned" you?
RICHIE. He just said, you know, you were ... a bit jumpy at the moment.
RACHEL. "Jumpy?"
RICHIE. Well he said things were, you know, a bit funny between you two at the moment. You know ... You're both working hard. You never see each other etcetera ... I mean ... he was quite frank about it. And I understand.
RACHEL. Frank about what?
RICHIE. He said you weren't ... communicating any more. That's all. He just said that there wasn't any ... communication at the moment. If you know what I mean. I mean ... you know Neal ... he likes to get things off his chest. He could've been a bit more discrete I suppose but ... what could I do? *(Silence.)*
RACHEL. Have I missed something?
RICHIE. Rachel, I wouldn't worry about it. You know what he's like. I've come from the other side of the world and Neal's decided to be boring about it. You know. Things change. People change. It's no big deal. *(Long pause.)*

RACHEL. Neal isn't boring.
RICHIE. He is. He's always been boring.
RACHEL. He isn't boring. He's just ... quieter than you.
RICHIE. A little shy and retiring. Absolutely.
RACHEL. Unpretentious.
RICHIE. Unpretentious and a little unadventurous sometimes ...
RACHEL. Perceptive.
RICHIE. Well absolutely. He thinks about things ...
RACHEL. He does. He's thoughtful ...
RICHIE. Earnest even. Humourless. And a little narrow-minded on occasions but only because he's so principled ...
RACHEL. He's just not like you.
RICHIE. No, absolutely. Absolutely. Enough said. *(Pause.)* Actually, he hasn't always been boring. When we were kids he was almost preternaturally fascinated by notions of playing "doctors and nurses."
RACHEL. Really? Who with?
RICHIE. Oh, some little floozy. Actually his next door neighbour. You know what kids are like ... It's a bit seedy really. Apparently they stripped completely naked one day and ... she showed him everything.
RACHEL. Neal?
RICHIE. They were on a climbing frame at the time ... I mean, he went into explicit detail about it. Frankly gynecological. *(Pause.)*
RACHEL. Then what happened?
RICHIE. Then he showed her everything. He's been almost uncontrollably titillated by the potential of role playing ever since.
RACHEL. Ridiculous.
RICHIE. So you see, he's really far more complex and charismatic than you think. *(Pause.)* Obviously I'd prefer it if you didn't mention it to him. He gets a bit jumpy when he thinks I've betrayed his confidence. *(Neal returns.)*
NEAL. They're filling up. We really have to make a move.
RICHIE. I haven't finished my drink.
RACHEL. I'm not hungry now.
NEAL. Well I'm starving.

RACHEL. Well I'm not.
RICHIE. Nor am I. I'm still thirsty.
NEAL. What do you mean you're not hungry?
RACHEL. I mean, I'm not hungry. I mean, I think I'd like another drink.
NEAL. What do you mean?
RACHEL. I mean I'd like another drink. I'm in the mood to drink. Drink and talk. You know. Communicate. *(Pause.)*
NEAL. Oh. Well ... *(He sits.)*
RICHIE. The most memorable drinking I ever did was in New York. Irish Bar called Malarchy's on 72nd and Columbus. The screwdrivers were like raw diazepam ...
NEAL. Have you ever heard of Wenicke-Korakoff's Syndrome?
RICHIE. No. Should I have?
NEAL. Alcoholics get it. One symptom is confabulation, otherwise known as inane chatter, often fabricated to present a legitimate, rather than untenable account of the recent past following memory loss. Another is depletion of social skills.
RICHIE. Could we have that in English?
NEAL. It means you can't shut up.
RICHIE. Well I never knew that before. How splendidly edifying. *(Silence. They drink.)*
RACHEL. I want to go to New York. I'd love to get smashed on screwdrivers in an Irish bar in Manhattan.
RICHIE. You wouldn't like it. It's all hairy-arsed commuters from Buffalo blowing their wages on baseball cards and hookers.
RACHEL. No I think I'd like it. You know, one day. When things aren't so funny between us. When I'm a little less jumpy about things perhaps.
NEAL. ... They have those places here now. In the Fulham Road.
RICHIE. Really?
NEAL. Yes.
RICHIE. How jolly.
RACHEL. We should give it a try some time. When I'm a little less jumpy about things. Once we've got through the rough patch. *(Neal looks at Rachel, then at Richie, then at Rachel again. Pause.)*

NEAL. Have I missed something?
RICHIE. Do they still have that place by the river with wagon wheels and the Wurlitzer? Very transatlantic. Very "go-go."
RACHEL. The Putney Star and Garter.
RICHIE. That's the one.
NEAL. ... I have lunch there when I'm at Queen Mary's. Has a rather nice view of the river ...
RICHIE. Perhaps we could have a spot of lunch there sometime?
RACHEL. I'd like that.
RICHIE. You could take a day off. Really let your hair down.
NEAL. You can't take a day off now.
RACHEL. At least entertain the notion Neal.
RICHIE. Yeah. Entertain the notion, Neal ...
RACHEL. How long are you staying?
RICHIE. How long can I stay?
RACHEL. How long do you want to stay?
RICHIE. Well ... long enough to have lunch at the Putney Star and Garter ... I mean, I wouldn't miss it for the world ...
NEAL. Look ... listen ... look ... listen ...
RACHEL. What's wrong? *(Pause.)*
NEAL. Never mind. *(Pause. They drink.)*
RICHIE. Isn't this marvelous? It's just so wonderful to be home. It really is nice. Who's for a short? Rachel?

Scene 4

Hospital. Morning. Neal sitting holding phone. Richie looking in the fridge.

NEAL. What's going on? I told you to put him through to my office ... Well I'm here now. Thank you ... I'm listening ... Jesus Christ ... Well it's not my fault ... Who else knows? I hope you didn't give them my name ... Why? *(Pause.)* Hello? *(He hangs up.)*
RICHIE. Problems?

NEAL. A heart bypass patient on a ventilator died last week during a power failure.
RICHIE. What happened to the back up generator?
NEAL. It didn't come on and the only person who knew how to switch it on was sick.
RICHIE. Ridiculous.
NEAL. Richie ...
RICHIE. The press is going to have a field day.
NEAL. I know ...
RICHIE. They should get their emergency procedure sorted out.
NEAL. I am the emergency procedure ... Look, what are you doing here? Stay away from that ... *(Richie shuts the fridge.)*
RICHIE. This happened when I was working for the Hammersmith *Recorder.* We thought it was Christmas. *(Richie retrieves the bottle of Scotch and pours. The phone rings. Neal picks it up.)*
NEAL. Yes? No press ... I am not qualified to make a statement to the press ... Find one of the consultants. *(Pause.)* Are they really in management meetings or are you just saying that? *(Pause.)* I'm not being churlish ... *(Pause.)* I have a right to be angry ... My nerves are shot ... I just want to be left alone ... I just want to do my job ... Will somebody please help me please? Hello? *(He hangs up. Silence.)*
RICHIE. You shouldn't get so wrapped up in it. Who cares?
NEAL. I have to be wrapped up in it. I have to care. I do care. More and more I don't want to. But there you go ...
RICHIE. I absolutely understand ... If you don't care enough you're a bad doctor and if you care too much you'll go insane and be no use to anyone etcetera. It's a dilemma. And the answer's very very simple.
NEAL. Well you'd better tell me then.
RICHIE. You're not cut out to be a doctor. Maybe you should try something a little less cut-throat. Like show business. *(Silence.)*
NEAL. This is my job. My thing. I like it.
RICHIE. Why?
NEAL. Because I can make a difference.
RICHIE. To who? *(Pause.)*
NEAL. I'm going to go berserk in a minute.

RICHIE. What is it? *(Pause.)* Is it lack of confidence? *(The phone rings. Richie picks it up.)*
NEAL. I'll take it.
RICHIE. *(Into phone.)* Yes? *(Neal reaches for the phone, Richie pulls it away.)*
NEAL. Give it to me.
RICHIE. *(Into phone.)* What do you want to know about it?
NEAL. My God. Who is it?
RICHIE. *(To Neal.)* Press office. *(Into phone.)* Now shut up and listen to me. Better still, take this down, you do have short hand don't you? There was a power failure, full stop. The back up generator was faulty and we're still investigating the cause of that fault, full stop.
NEAL. Richie please ...
RICHIE. *(Into phone.)* Fortunately the day to day running of the hospital was not unduly affected and of the few patients on ventilators none came to any harm, full stop new paragraph ...
NEAL. I'm begging you ...
RICHIE. *(Into phone.)* Unfortunately, comma, in a part of the hospital which was not affected, comma, one patient recovering from a life-threatening illness passed away during the night. Full stop close quotes.
NEAL. Fuck ...
RICHIE. *(Into phone.)* He just died in the night. *(Pause.)* It's a coincidence. *(Richie hangs up abruptly. Neal sits with his head in his hands.)*
RACHEL. Are you all right?
NEAL. It's unethical.
RICHIE. It's standard practice.
NEAL. It's amoral.
RICHIE. We had no choice. There's no point in you sticking your neck out.
NEAL. A man died. The least we can do is tell the truth.
RICHIE. Don't be ridiculous.
NEAL. What about the family? We can't lie to his family.
RICHIE. Will you just dry up?
NEAL. We are complicit ... we are complicit now in a moral felony.

RICHIE. A moral what? *(He laughs.)*
NEAL. Will you listen to me?
RICHIE. Are you hungry?
NEAL. Why are you like this?
RICHIE. Why are you like this? Moan moan moan ... honestly. You've had a nice suburban upbringing. Loving parents. Educated at one of the finest comprehensives in Wolverhampton. Good job, nice flat, sexy girlfriend. You're practically a blueprint for mindless contentment, but you're still not happy, are you?
NEAL. ... I'm perfectly happy. *(Richie retrieves the bottle of Scotch. Pours. They drink.)*
RICHIE. Neal, everything's going to be all right. Everybody has these doubts.
NEAL. I see a psychiatrist friend once a month. He says I suffer from anxiety. As a favour, he doesn't invoice me, but I pay him anyway because it's against my principals.
RICHIE. You really suffer from anxiety? That surprises me.
NEAL. It's nothing.
RICHIE. You'll burn yourself out.
NEAL. I don't want to talk about it. *(Pause.)* You have your problems. I have mine.
RICHIE. I've never had to resort to psychiatric help.
NEAL. Maybe you should. Now leave me alone. *(Richie exits.)*

Scene 5

Bedroom. Night. Rachel and Neal lounging on the bed. Moonlight from a window.

RACHEL. Isn't the moon beautiful? And the sunset. Wasn't the sunset lovely tonight? Golden. It didn't look like England. Didn't look like London. The common, rinsed in sunlight ... Gorgeous.

NEAL. He met the dean of the medical school today. In the cafeteria. Kept calling him James and laughing.
RACHEL. Don't worry about it.
NEAL. He's a clown. A misfit.
RACHEL. He's just a bit lost, that's all.
NEAL. Do you know why he spends his life traveling around the world? Because nobody can bear him at home.
RACHEL. He did you a favour.
NEAL. He lied.
RACHEL. He was being economical with the truth.
NEAL. One of my patients died.
RACHEL. They die all the time and it wasn't your fault. If he hadn't done what he did you would have swung for it.
NEAL. I know. But I can't help feeling that something terrible is going to happen. Something inexplicable and insidious and ... unexpected. I mean — where's it going to end? What next?
RACHEL. You're very stressed at the moment. It's just anxiety.
NEAL. Is it? Is it really?
RACHEL. Yes. *(She kisses him chastely.)* He told me a funny story about you. He said that as a child you had a thing about playing "doctors and nurses."
NEAL. How do you mean?
RACHEL. He said there was this little girl who you became intimately familiar with on a climbing frame.
NEAL. He did, did he?
RACHEL. I thought it was quite sweet.
NEAL. It's nonsense. It's a lie.
RACHEL. It's a rather charming one.
NEAL. I hate it when he does that. He's so ... mendacious.
RACHEL. Well, I dare say it's fairly harmless.
NEAL. It's stupid. It's just stupid ...
RACHEL. I wouldn't lose any sleep over it.
NEAL. No. No of course not. That would be playing right into his hands. *(Silence.)*
RACHEL. Do you remember when I lived in Kilburn?
NEAL. Vaguely.
RACHEL. Oh you do. You remember. Things were fun in those days. Everything was fun. Just going out for a takeaway was

fun. Spectacularly engrossing. We did a lot of sitting about on the floor with candles I seem to remember. We'd lie in bed for hours and hours and light candles and talk long into the night.
NEAL.   Mm.
RACHEL.   I mean we really talked. Long, long into the night. Very intense long chats.
NEAL.   What about?
RACHEL.   Oh, all sorts of things. Books, films, where we wanted to go, what we wanted to do with our lives. We'd just talk. Laugh. Giggle. Tell each other stories. You know, communicate. *(She kisses him.)* Let's go away somewhere.
NEAL.   Where do you want to go?
RACHEL.   I don't know. Prague. Thailand. Leeds.
NEAL.   I don't want to go anywhere. I want him to go.
RACHEL.   What about me?
NEAL.   You know holidays make me nervous. It's the leaving that's the worst part ...
RACHEL.   And the coming home ...
NEAL.   Airports make me nervous ...
RACHEL.   And all that time in between ...
NEAL.   I can't stop thinking about work.
RACHEL.   It could be worse. Look at Richie. He's haunted.
NEAL.   No. He's just confused.
RACHEL.   I think it's interesting. A "dark side."
NEAL.   I'm haunted.
RACHEL.   No. You're just a worrier.
NEAL.   What do I worry about?
RACHEL.   Everything. Every thought you have has an intrinsically lugubrious, sensitive quality. It's just the type of person you are. I like it.
NEAL.   Really?
RACHEL.   Absolutely. *(Pause.)*
NEAL.   That's just what I like about you. The quality of your thoughts is entirely different. Generous and unassuming. You're an extremely positive person but not in a relentless, thrusting way.
RACHEL.   I like the way you worry about things. Some people never worry about anything and that's just boring. *(Pause.)*

NEAL. I like these conversations. I feel better already.
RACHEL. My darling. I'll look after you ...
NEAL. I'll look after you ...
RACHEL. I don't need looking after.
NEAL. What do you need?
RACHEL. I don't need anything. A ticket to Thailand would be nice. *(Pause.)*
NEAL. See, now this is what worries me.
RACHEL. Why?
NEAL. Because it exemplifies precisely what I was talking about. I should be happy that you're so adventurous and independent but I'd prefer it if you needed more attention.
RACHEL. Maybe I do. Maybe we both do. *(Pause.)*
NEAL. You know, it's become my aim in life to become more like you. I'd rather I became more like you as we grew old than you became like me.
RACHEL. Me too. Definitely.
NEAL. Maybe that's how marriage works. You become more like each other. Given the right proximity and exposure, people rub off on each other. And I want you to rub off on me.
RACHEL. I want you to rub off on me too. *(Pause.)*
NEAL. I mean, I'd love to be married to you. I'd get a big bang out of that.
RACHEL. Me too. You know. One day ... *(Pause.)*
NEAL. We're never bored with each other. We never argue. No weirdness or complexity has so far manifested and maybe never will. Maybe we're immune. I think we are. We are. We're immune. *(Pause.)* Have we just proposed to each other? *(Silence. Richie is standing in the doorway, watching. Neal watches Richie. Neal pulls the sheet over Rachel. Rachel turns and sees Richie.)*
RACHEL. Hi.
RICHIE. Hi-ya. *(Pause.)* I was looking for the bathroom.
RACHEL. It's next door. I'll show you.
NEAL. It's next door. You can't miss it. *(Richie goes.)* Did you see that?
RACHEL. What?
NEAL. The way he just stood there, staring.

RACHEL. I didn't see.
NEAL. He was standing there staring. For ages. Without saying anything.
RACHEL. He was probably embarrassed.
NEAL. He wasn't embarrassed. He was enjoying himself.
RACHEL. I don't think so.
NEAL. He was staring right at you. Gazing at your naked arse.
RACHEL. Why would he do that?
NEAL. Why do you think?
RACHEL. Don't be ridiculous.
NEAL. I'm not being ridiculous. You're being ... He was ...
RACHEL. What? Just don't worry about it.
NEAL. I'm not worried about it ...
RACHEL. Well just forget about it ...
NEAL. All right, it's forgotten.
RACHEL. This is our time now. You and me. Alone. Together ...
NEAL. I know. Absolutely ... *(Pause.)*
RACHEL. What shall we do now?
NEAL. He knows where the bathroom is. I showed him.
RACHEL. Maybe he forgot ...
NEAL. No. You don't forget a thing like that.
RACHEL. Oh Neal ...
NEAL. You don't believe me do you?
RACHEL. Don't be silly. I just think ...
NEAL. I'm not being silly. You're being ...
RACHEL. What?
NEAL. I hate to say it but ...
RACHEL. Well don't say it then. *(Pause.)*
NEAL. I just think you're being a bit ... naive.
RACHEL. Naive?
NEAL. I think you are.
RACHEL. Neal, for goodness sake. He probably didn't know what to say.
NEAL. He was watching us. Watching you.
RACHEL. So what?
NEAL. So what? *(Pause.)* So what? *(Pause.)* So, I don't like it, that's what. *(He rolls over. Blackout.)*

Scene 6

Neal and Rachel's flat. Early morning. Richie face down on the floor, clutching a whisky bottle. Neal standing, tying his tie.

NEAL. What are you doing today? *(Pause. He prods Richie with his foot.)* Wake up Richie. *(He slaps Richie's face.)* What have you done? *(He looks on the floor and picks up a syringe and vial.)* You stupid prick. *(He slaps Richie's face quickly. Rachel enters with a towel around her, hair wet.)*
RACHEL. What's all this row about?
NEAL. He's knocked himself out with ketamine.
RACHEL. Christ. I'll get my bag. *(Neal finds Richie's pulse.)*
NEAL. Ring the hospital and tell then to send a resuscitation unit and an airway. They might need an IV so tell them to get one ready. *(Rachel goes to the phone and dials. Richie blinks and looks around. Rachel puts the phone down.)*
RACHEL. Thank God.
NEAL. Where did you get this from ... He's caned ... This is a serious general anaesthetic. I use it in the operating theatre. It's the closest thing you can do to killing someone and if you don't know how to do it you do kill them.
RICHIE. And you can buy it off grannies on any Moscow street corner. Relax.
NEAL. You might as well do smack.
RICHIE. Oh I do smack all the time. The whole trip, man. Sometimes I wear an upside down crucifix I bought in Berlin and paint my fingernails black for parties.
NEAL. If I was caught using this in my home I'd go to prison.
RICHIE. I'd visit you.
NEAL. They could've been stolen from my doctor's bag. Or my supply fridge. From right under my nose ...
RACHEL. You're not helping, Neal ...
RICHIE. Are you accusing me? Me? Of all people...?
NEAL. Yes.

RICHIE. Then you've got the balls of King Kong. I'm flabbergasted. *(Pause.)* I'm fucking astonished. *(Pause.)* All right. I pinched it. Shoot me.
NEAL. Don't you understand? One of these days they'll cart you into my hospital on a stretcher and I'll have to save your life.
RICHIE. Well I hope you know what you're doing.
NEAL. Don't you think I have enough to contend with? *(Richie sits up.)* How much have you got left?
RICHIE. Nothing.
NEAL. How much Richie?
RICHIE. Five mill.
NEAL. It's not funny, I've got problems.
RICHIE. Have you?
NEAL. Either it's me or it's you. I honestly can't tell anymore. *(Richie produces the ketamine. Hands it over.)* Wouldn't you say that you've gone far enough or are there depths you still haven't sunk to yet?
RICHIE. I'd say that I've seen God and I want to see him again.
NEAL. You probably will.
RACHEL. Well, it's done now. What's done is done.
NEAL. What do you think would happen if every time they wheeled in somebody with a crushed skull and punctured lungs they got you and you said, "It's done now. What's done is done?" Eh? Think about it.
RACHEL. Look, you're just getting a little ...
NEAL. A little what? Anxious?
RACHEL. Yes.
NEAL. Fine. *(Pause.)* Anxious, fine. *(Pause.)* Over-anxious or just anxious?
RACHEL. You don't have to get uptight with me.
NEAL. I'm sorry. I'm sorry but ...
RACHEL. But what? *(Pause)* Just don't do it Neal. It's not nice.
NEAL. I'm sorry ...
RACHEL. OK? *(Rachel exits to the bedroom.)*
RICHIE. You've done it now. She's upset. I can tell. *(Pause.)* It's the silent treatment for you for a while. I bet she's good at

the silent treatment, that one. I expect you'll have to go in there and make it up to her now. Go and cheer her up. Go and give her a good thorough cheering up. A good, long, hard cheering up.
NEAL.   When are you going to leave us alone?
RICHIE.   Sorry?
NEAL.   I mean I've had enough and I want you out of here now.
RICHIE.   Well you'll have to lend me the money. *(Neal produces money and gives it to Richie.)* Are you sure you don't want to talk to Rachel about this?
NEAL.   She wants you out. She told me.
RICHIE.   Are you sure?
NEAL.   As soon as you've found a hotel.
RICHIE.   That could take some time.
NEAL.   That's not my problem. It's your problem. Understand? *(Pause.)* And I'd appreciate it if at some point in the future you stop telling your libidinous, vaguely deranged childhood stories about me.
RICHIE.   I don't know what you're talking about.
NEAL.   That childish story about my playing "doctors and nurses." You were telling that at school. You just haven't changed have you?
RICHIE.   Sometimes I vary it.
NEAL.   What?
RICHIE.   Sometimes it's "firemen."
NEAL.   You're sick.
RICHIE.   I did you a favour. At least now she thinks you're interesting, instead of spending the rest of her life only seeing you as the mincing, leftie, goody-goody jobsworth you really are. I wish I had a friend who'd do that for me.
NEAL.   You don't have any friends.
RICHIE.   There's no need to get personal. *(Rachel returns wearing a towelling robe and fills the kettle.)* Are you going to work now?
NEAL.   We're not leaving you here by yourself.
RACHEL.   He can stay if he likes. I'm taking the day off.

NEAL. Why?
RACHEL. I'm not feeling well.
NEAL. What's wrong with you?
RACHEL. I don't know. I just don't want to go to work.
RICHIE. Nothing wrong with that. *(Pause.)*
RACHEL. I'm just run down.
NEAL. Let me feel your glands. *(He goes to feel her glands, she pushes him away.)*
RACHEL. Oh, get off me ... *(Rachel goes back to the bedroom and slams the door.)*
RICHIE. Hysterical ...
NEAL. Now what have I done?
RICHIE. I love it when she scolds you. I like a good scolding ...
NEAL. What did I do? *(Silence.)*
RICHIE. Neal, I really don't want to cause any problems.

Scene 7

River. Afternoon. Richie and Rachel walking. Rachel holds a bunch of cornflowers.

RICHIE. I fancy a swim.
RACHEL. You can't swim in the river. You'll get meningitis.
RICHIE. Who cares?
RACHEL. You know, we shouldn't have done that. I'm feeling a bit pissed. *(Richie belches.)*
RICHIE. What was that place called? I don't like that place.
RACHEL. Which one?
RICHIE. The first one. The Moon one. On the Green.
RACHEL. It's called the Moon on the Green.
RICHIE. And did we? *(They chuckle. They stop and soak up the sun.)*
RACHEL. This is what your day off should be about. What's wrong with the occasional afternoon in the pub? What's wrong

with the occasional sickie? What's wrong with the occasional ... lie?
RICHIE.   It's contra to the Hippocratic oath.
RACHEL.   I spend my days off studying mental patients in Springfield. Then there's the crack-ups at the Maudsley. I might join them soon if I don't get a holiday.
RICHIE.   No. Not you.
RACHEL.   I just wish it was like it was before. Before we graduated, before you went away, before any of us knew anything. I want Neal to come away with me. Ditch the mortgage and the job and vanish. No work, no responsibilities, just us and the backpacks.
RICHIE.   Where?
RACHEL.   Get an around the world ticket, go wherever we feel like.
RICHIE.   And give up everything you've worked for?
RACHEL.   Oh, what's the point? Every day at the crack of dawn I float off down the High Street in the freezing cold to get on a crammed tube to go and treat the angina and asthma of chain-smokers, cancer referrals, local schizophrenics who nobody has the nerve to diagnose ... there's no cure for any of it.
RICHIE.   You're right. Sounds like a drag.
RACHEL.   But you've been places, you've met interesting people. You had an exciting career.
RICHIE.   I wasn't very good at it.
RACHEL.   I don't believe that. Why all the stories then?
RICHIE.   What does Neal think about all this?
RACHEL.   I may go without him.
RICHIE.   Really?
RACHEL.   What else can I do? You're right. He can be a very boring person.
RICHIE.   Don't say that.
RACHEL.   I don't mean to be nasty but ...
RICHIE.   No go on. I'm listening ... It's unusual to find somebody so well-balanced with such a low opinion of people.
RACHEL.   I'm not that well-balanced. I'm quite flighty when I want to be.
RICHIE.   I like flighty women. Flighty women are great. *(Pause.)*

RACHEL. Do you think I'm naive?
RICHIE. How do you mean?
RACHEL. Naive. I'm naive, aren't I?
RICHIE. No.
RACHEL. I think about it sometimes. In the wee small hours. In the "dark night of the soul ..." *(Pause.)*
RICHIE. In the dark night of the soul you think that you're naive?
RACHEL. I do.
RICHIE. Really? So do I.
RACHEL. Do you?
RICHIE. In the dark night of the soul I think that I'm naive. All the time.
RACHEL. Sometimes I think it's naive to expect to be ... you know ... happy.
RICHIE. So do I.
RACHEL. But it's not naivete. It's just being ... optimistic. Hopeful.
RICHIE. Quietly hopeful in the face of ... overwhelming odds.
RACHEL. Expectant.
RICHIE. Quietly expectant. Absolutely.
RACHEL. Idealistic ...
RICHIE. Quixotic even ...
RACHEL. What does that mean?
RICHIE. It means that ... you're not naive. In fact it means the exact opposite of naive. I mean, you know, you have a certain innocence ... but there's nothing wrong with that. I mean you're innocent but at the same time ... extremely shrewd ... I like it. *(Silence.)*
RACHEL. We should go back I suppose.
RICHIE. Do you want another drink?
RACHEL. You're terrible.
RICHIE. I know. But I've got an excuse.
RACHEL. What?
RICHIE. I can't help it.
RACHEL. That's what's terrible.
RACHEL. Hey. You'll like this. A horse walks into a bar and orders a beer. What does the barman say to the horse?

RACHEL. Richie ...
RICHIE. Come on, what does the barman say? *(Silence.)* Do you want me to go? *(Pause.)*
RACHEL. Do you want me to be honest? *(Pause.)*
RICHIE. Not particularly.
RACHEL. I think it's for the best. *(Pause.)*
RICHIE. I'm going to Wales next. I've already decided. Don't try and talk me out of it ...
RACHEL. Wales is lovely. Neal and I used to go to the Pembrokeshire Coast. Tenby.
RICHIE. *(Accent.)* Tenby? Tidy.
RACHEL. *(Accent.)* Not so bad ... Wales.
RICHIE. Boats, seagulls, fish and chips, cliffs. I like cliffs. It'll be brilliant. I'll rent a room. They're dirt cheap in winter, can't give them away.
RACHEL. It's not winter.
RICHIE. I know.
RACHEL. You'll be bored out of your mind.
RICHIE. I know. *(Silence.)* I had a dream last night. We were by the sea.
RACHEL. We?
RICHIE. Not in England ... Thailand perhaps ... It was warm and the sky was purple and we were eating sea urchins. It was like a beach party. A clambake, like in the Elvis movie, *Clambake*. We all had to find a bit of seafood and cook it. You and me were a team, and we couldn't find any, so we went up to this fellow and pinched his sea urchins. Then we cooked them and we were eating them, just us, sitting on the shore in the dark, watching the stars, just absorbing the brilliance and beauty and inky wonder of it all. I had a pounding headache and as if by magic, you turned the sea urchins into ice cream. And then I ate the ice cream and my headache went. What do you think it means?
RACHEL. Nothing probably. The good ones are usually meaningless.
RICHIE. No, seriously. You did Freud and Jung and all that Viennese argy-bargy. Why sea-urchins?
RACHEL. Well ... It's obviously bollocks, isn't it?
RICHIE. I think it means something.

RACHEL. No, that's what it means. Freud would say you had a thing about testicles and Jung would say you saw yourself as a testicle. Don't ask me about the ice cream though. *(Pause.)* Maybe it means you always want something you can't have. Something that's metaphysically-speaking not on the menu.
RICHIE. Nicky?
RACHEL. You're always looking for somebody or something to make the unpalatable palatable. Maybe only Nicky can do that for you. *(Pause.)*
RICHIE. It's the not knowing that does my head in. Not knowing where she is, whether she's all right ... Who she's with ... I feel excluded ... She hasn't even rung. Why hasn't she rung?
RACHEL. She doesn't know where you are.
RICHIE. She could find out.
RACHEL. How?
RICHIE. She could guess. *(Pause. Rachel pats his arm.)*
RACHEL. Thanks for the flowers. Neal bought me flowers once. I told him I didn't like flowers and he never bought me them again.
RICHIE. Well, do you?
RACHEL. Yes. They're lovely. *(Pause. They look at each other. He tries to kiss her — she avoids. He tries again.)* Richie ...
RICHIE. I've been thinking.
RACHEL. What are you thinking?
RICHIE. I think about you all the time. I've tried to put you out of my mind. I thought it was just lust ... but it's more than that.
RACHEL. Don't be silly ...
RICHIE. We understand each other.
RACHEL. Do we...?
RICHIE. When I'm with you, I'm watching fireworks. When I'm with you I am a firework. Electricity pulses through my veins. Moonbeams dazzle my eyes and I'm blinded. Delighted. Enchanted ... When I'm not with you I walk about lost, staring, talking to myself, my shirt is on back to front, my fly's undone, my trousers falling down, hollow, completely hollow. I want to preach the gospel according to Us. Yell it from the rooftops. From a multistory car park ... I'm not making myself plain, am

I...? I think you're lovely. You are the word lovely on two lovely legs. We'll be a knockout together. We'll be Butch Cassidy and the Sundance Kid. We'll be the Cisco Kid and Pancho. We'll be the King and Queen of Happiness. It's entirely possible. I'm not afraid of looking ridiculous. I'm not afraid of anything. I mean business. *(Long pause.)*

RACHEL.　Sorry...? I didn't catch that ...
RICHIE.　Come and live with me in Wales.
RACHEL.　With you? You?
RICHIE.　Yes. Me.
RACHEL.　What about Neal?
RICHIE.　Oh, fuck Neal. Look at you. The way you look away. The way you go quiet ...
RACHEL.　This is embarrassing ...
RICHIE.　The way you get embarrassed ... *(He kisses her.)*
RACHEL.　What are you doing you ... you idiot. Oh, you fool ... *(He holds her, squeezes her ardently. She breaks away.)* Will you stop doing that? I love Neal. We've got a mortgage ... It's serious.
RICHIE.　You said you were bored with Neal.
RACHEL.　I am ... I'm not ...
RICHIE.　Make up your mind. What do you want?
RACHEL.　I don't know what I want. *(Pause.)* Neither do you. You're just drunk.
RICHIE.　So are you. *(She goes. Blackout.)*

ACT TWO

Scene 1

French Restaurant. Evening. Neal, Rachel and Richie at a table drinking wine.

NEAL. *(Drunk.)* How much time was spent pouring over ethics when we were at medical school? Eh? How many fruitless hours, weeks, months in the students' union bar bickering over, I don't know, euthanasia or something. It was the same in community medicine. Polygamy this, termination that ... Taxing the moral reserves of ... students? It's pointless. The most unfeeling ones just join health authorities and become bloody managers. *(Richie yawns.)* Nobody cares. Nobody understands. Nobody wants to understand. *(Pause.)* You see what I mean?
RACHEL. Sorry? I wasn't listening.
NEAL. Medical ethics I'm talking about.
RACHEL. Oh. I never listened during medical ethics.
RICHIE. Do you think that snails have the same aphrodisiac qualities as oysters?
RACHEL. I thought you had frog legs.
RICHIE. It tasted like chicken. How was the duck?
RACHEL. The chocolate sauce was gorgeous.
NEAL. I'm a very bad doctor. I am. It's as simple as that.
RICHIE. I've got one. A horse walks into a bar and orders a beer. What does the barman say to the horse? *(Pause.)* "Why the long face?" *(Silence.)* I need to piss. *(He leaves the table.)*
NEAL. Do you think he knows he's an alcoholic?
RACHEL. Yes I do. *(Pause.)*

NEAL. You don't think he's ...
RACHEL. What?
NEAL. In the toilet ... injecting.
RACHEL. I don't know. How should I know? *(Pause.)*
NEAL. I'm sorry. This must be very strange for you. Things really have got a little out of hand.
RACHEL. Things have got very out of hand.
NEAL. That's Richie for you. There's a lot of things you don't know about him.
RACHEL. Such as?
NEAL. All sorts of things.
RACHEL. What?
NEAL. Well ... He's mad isn't he? I'm sure there's a few things I don't know either. *(Pause.)* I wanted us to be alone tonight. I needed to talk to you.
RACHEL. What about?
NEAL. Anything. I just needed to talk. Ask you if you're all right. Tell you I love you.
RACHEL. I love you too. *(Neal pours a glass of wine and drinks.)*
NEAL. *(Drunken.)* See, I have this theory about love ... Our minds are like the doors to a lift in a tall building. And our hearts are behind those doors. And when we fall in love, we throw open our doors, and let all our feelings out, and all the other person's feelings in and ... Our souls hold hands and romp naked together ... free. *(Pause.)* No ... we're the lifts and our hearts are ... No ... there's all these buttons, see ... and we push them ... *(Pause.)* And then we either go up or we go down. Shall we order cheese? *(Silence.)* How are you feeling?
RACHEL. I'm just tired.
NEAL. You're always tired ...
RICHIE. What does that mean?
NEAL. It doesn't mean anything. I'm concerned. Perhaps it's narcolepsy. *(Pause.)* It doesn't mean anything. I just wish you'd tell me what's on your mind. *(Pause.)* You never moan about anything.
RACHEL. He ... made a pass at me this morning. Cheeky bugger.
NEAL. What?

RACHEL. We went for a walk by the river and he lunged.
NEAL. He lunged?
RACHEL. It was nothing. He squeezed my breast.
NEAL. My God. Are you sure?
RACHEL. As sure as I can be. It was definitely my breast.
NEAL. My God. Are you sure he wasn't just ...
RACHEL. Just what?
NEAL. Giving you a hug or something?
RACHEL. I'm fairly certain, Neal. He didn't mean it. He was drunk.
NEAL. That shouldn't make any difference. He's always drunk.
RACHEL. I dealt with it. It's no big deal.
NEAL. It is a big deal. That's very extreme behavior Rachel. I'll kill him. *(Neal pours more wine and drinks thirstily. Rachel takes his hand.)*
RACHEL. Don't say any more, Neal. And don't you dare mention it to him.
NEAL. I bloody well will. There's a principle at stake.
RACHEL. Don't be so pedantic.
NEAL. Pedantic?
RACHEL. You are. You're pedantic.
NEAL. No. No I'm not. Particular maybe, but that's not pedantry. There's a distinct difference ... Is there or isn't there a difference...? *(Richie returns. Pause.)*
RICHIE. Anyone for pud?
NEAL. I think you've had yours. Or rather mine.
RACHEL. I've had quite enough for one evening.
NEAL. Shall we ask for the bill?
RACHEL. Mm. *(Neal tries to catch the waiter's eye, unsuccessfully. Richie snaps his fingers.)*
RICHIE. Garçon! *(Pause. To Rachel.)* Your turn.
RACHEL. Oh, this is ridiculous. *(She gets up.)*
RICHIE. Flutter your eyelashes at him. *(She goes to find the waiter. Pause.)*
NEAL. Listen, old chap ... *(Neal sips his wine.)*
RICHIE. What's wrong, old chap?
NEAL. This is going to sound ... absurd ... but I think you owe Rachel an apology.

RICHIE. Why?
NEAL. I just think things have been getting a little bit out of hand.
RICHIE. In what way?
NEAL. The ... you know ... the flirting.
RICHIE. Flirting? *(Pause.)*
NEAL. Oh come off it Richie. You've been flirting with her ever since you arrived.
RICHIE. Flirting? Me?
NEAL. And the rest.
RICHIE. What?
NEAL. I know what happened. Between you two. By the river. *(Pause.)*
RICHIE. Mate. I have no idea what you're talking about.
NEAL. I think you do.
RICHIE. I don't. What's happened? *(Pause.)*
NEAL. This is going to sound silly ... but Rachel said something happened by the river. You gave her a hug or something and ...
RICHIE. A hug?
NEAL. Mm.
RICHIE. Well I probably did. Just to cheer her up, you know ... *(Pause.)*
NEAL. I see. OK.
RICHIE. Why?
NEAL. I don't know. I think ... maybe she took it the wrong way.
RICHIE. She took it the wrong way you say?
NEAL. She says you squeezed her breast. *(Richie looks round-eyed.)*
RICHIE. Whaaat?
NEAL. That's what she said. And I hate that I have to ... tell tales but ...
RICHIE. She said I squeezed her breast? *(Neal nods. Pause.)*
RICHIE. Hard?
NEAL. I've no idea. *(Pause.)*
RICHIE. Which breast?

NEAL. Listen, you might have, you know, pinched her bum or something ... in a friendly way, you know, in a you know, a cheeky way ...
RICHIE. Are you sure she meant me?
NEAL. She was fairly specific.
RICHIE. Then I'm shocked. I'm hurt. Really.
NEAL. Don't tell me this is ... a complete surprise?
RICHIE. Yes.
NEAL. Oh. *(Pause.)* Really?
RICHIE. The bitch.
NEAL. Look, she didn't even want me to mention it ...
RICHIE. I'll be she didn't. No wonder she didn't ...
NEAL. Look, something must have happened.
RICHIE. She's a very uptight girl, Neal. I thought even you knew that.
NEAL. What do you mean?
RICHIE. Oh come on. All this "Wanderlust." All this "My life is so dull and regimented ..." She's a lovely girl Neal. I've always liked her and respected her and what's more I think her sensitivity is good for you ... but she's needy. She's clingy. Insecure. I bet she's Catholic. Is she Catholic Neal? Because I hate to invoke stereotypes but ... sometimes you have to.
NEAL. ... No. She isn't. *(Silence.)* Why would she make it up, Rich?
RICHIE. Why?
NEAL. Yes. *(Pause.)*
RICHIE. Because she's a liar.
NEAL. You're a liar.
RICHIE. I'd never lie to you.
NEAL. You always lie to me.
RICHIE. I'd never lie about a thing like this.
NEAL. Neither would she.
RICHIE. Well neither would I. Can't you see what she's trying to do? It's the oldest trick in the book.
NEAL. Now what are you on about?
RICHIE. She's jealous.
NEAL. Of what?

RICHIE. Of what?
NEAL. Yes. *(Pause.)*
RICHIE. Well if you don't know, I'm not going to tell you ...
NEAL. Tell me. I'm interested.
RICHIE. Because we're such good friends, obviously.
NEAL. Look ... Just tell me the truth for once.
RICHIE. I've told you the truth.
NEAL. Swear on your mother's life.
RICHIE. And my father's. Gladly. *(Pause.)* Is that it? Because, you know, if there's something on your mind, you can always talk to me. *(Rachel returns to the table, sits.)*
RACHEL. I put it on my card. You didn't want coffee did you?
RICHIE. I'll find a cab. *(Richie goes. Pause.)*
NEAL. Look. This is the last I'm going to say on the subject ...
RACHEL. Oh please ...
NEAL. But I'm in a dilemma ...
RACHEL. What's the dilemma? It was nothing, insignificant.
NEAL. He denies all knowledge of it. Completely denies it.
RACHEL. Well are you surprised?
NEAL. Yes. It's like he has amnesia.
RACHEL. Maybe he does. *(Pause.)*
NEAL. You think he just ... doesn't remember? *(Pause.)* No. You don't forget a thing like this. Are you sure about all this?
RACHEL. What are you implying Neal?
NEAL. I'm not implying anything. I just want to get to the bottom of it.
RACHEL. Well you're starting to sound ... suspicious of me.
NEAL. I'm not. What's there to be suspicious of? Suspicious? *(Pause.)* I'm just saying ... why didn't you tell me before? Eh? What else haven't you told me?
RACHEL. Oh just forget about it will you?
NEAL. All right. It's forgotten. I won't say another word. *(Silence.)* I really think we should talk about this ... *(Pause.)* He's my best friend. He's my oldest friend.
RACHEL. Oh I wish I'd never mentioned it now ... *(She sips her wine. Pause.)*
NEAL. Why?
RACHEL. Sweet Jesus Neal. Why are you so jumpy about everything.

NEAL. Jumpy?
RACHEL. Jumpy, yes. You're a very jumpy person.
NEAL. Jumpy? I used to be sensitive ... Now I'm just jumpy.
RACHEL. I used to think I knew you. Really knew you ... And then you start acting like this and ... Sometimes I don't think I know you at all. *(Silence.)*
NEAL. I worked a hundred hours this week. One hundred hours.
RACHEL. So did I. *(Pause.)*
NEAL. For three years I've been languishing in that diabolical place, pushing shit up hill, postponing one crisis after another, or stuck behind a desk, studying, or writing reports. I could be at the Chelsea and Westminster if I kissed the right arses. It's all tennis elbow and people falling over at barbecues there.
RACHEL. You can't afford to let it get to you.
NEAL. Why not?
RACHEL. Because it's getting to me. *(Neal pours another Scotch and drinks.)*
NEAL. I'm nearly thirty and my skin's never seen the sun and I suffer from anxiety and all I'm thinking is, somebody else is having all the fun. I'm thinking people like him are having all the fun. Even when he's not having fun he does it better than me. I've wasted my entire life! *(Silence.)* I'll go and see where that cab's got to. *(He goes. Rachel finishes off the wine. She stares. Richie returns and sits.)*
RICHIE. I'll be about ten minutes.
RACHEL. What?
RICHIE. The cab. I phoned for one in the end. Less arsing about.
RACHEL. What did you say to Neal about this morning?
RICHIE. This morning?
RACHEL. By the river.
RICHIE. Absolutely nothing. Why?
RACHEL. It doesn't matter. *(Pause.)*
RICHIE. Well ... I told him I bought you a bunch of flowers to cheer you up and I think it ... cheesed him off a bit.
RACHEL. Why would it "cheese" him off?
RICHIE. He thinks I was moving in on his territory.
RACHEL. You were.

RICHIE. I know but he doesn't know that. Flowers could mean anything. He doesn't even buy you flowers, how the hell would he know? *(Pause.)*
RACHEL. He said you completely denied it, Richie.
RICHIE. I didn't get a chance to deny it. You know what he's like. *(Pause.)* Look, I told him I gave you a hug. He told me you'd taken it the wrong way. He said you always did.
RACHEL. Always did what?
RICHIE. Took it the wrong way. With men.
RACHEL. What?
RICHIE. It's pathetic.
RACHEL. Right, that's it ...
RICHIE. He's just a bit insecure. You're an extremely sexy woman. I don't know if you're aware of it.
RACHEL. Will you please just...? *(Pause.)* Extremely sexy woman ... indeed ...
RICHIE. Look, it's human nature. People always take it out on the ones they love. *(Pause.)* And ... even if they don't really love them. People are cruel. *(Pause.)* And there's no explanation for any of it. *(Richie pours a glass of wine for Rachel and one for himself. He drinks.)* Think about it. Why do you love Neal so much? Why do you yearn for him when he's not around? Why are you so hungry just to talk to him, to hold him, to have him hold you when you're all worn out and just want some tenderness at the end of a long, hard day. Why do you love him so?
RACHEL. Beats me.
RICHIE. Because you love him. Because you just do. And it's glorious. And nothing else matters. And that's the way it should be or heaven help us all. That's the way it should be or you're in serious motherfucking trouble.
RACHEL. I think I take your point. *(Silence. Neal returns.)*
NEAL. I found a cab.
RICHIE. There's one coming. Little firm I know, on the cheap.
NEAL. What, a minicab?
RACHEL. Oh Neal don't be such a prick. *(Silence. Neal goes.)* I know what you're trying to do, Richie.
RICHIE. What am I trying to do?

RACHEL. I've seen this act before. I think it's a sign of serious psychological unbalance.
RICHIE. Yeah? And what's this a sign of? *(He propels Rachel onto the table.)*
RACHEL. Are you listening to me...? I mean it ...
RICHIE. Then why don't you do something about it, doctor? *(He holds her down and kisses her.)*
RACHEL. Don't
RICHIE. Shut up.
RACHEL. Not in here.
RICHIE. Why the hell not? *(She pushes him away. Pause. They embrace and kiss.)*

Scene 2

Neal and Rachel's flat. Evening. Richie and Rachel sitting up in bed. Rachel stares. Lit candles dotted about the room.

RACHEL. What's wrong?
RICHIE. Opening night nerves. *(Pause.)* Too much to drink. *(Pause.)* I'm shy. *(She strokes him under the covers.)* Rachel ... *(She stops.)* Give it a rest, eh?
RACHEL. I was enjoying myself.
RICHIE. It's perfectly normal. Frank Sinatra said it means you just haven't got to know the lady properly yet. *(Pause.)* I'm nervous.
RACHEL. Did you mean what you said by the river yesterday?
RICHIE. When?
RACHEL. You know.
RICHIE. Oh that. Of course I did.
RACHEL. You kept it pretty quiet.
RICHIE. There's a lot of things you don't know about me Rachel.

RACHEL. I know. Neal told me you couldn't even do shorthand.
RICHIE. What?
RACHEL. He said they sent you on a course with a bunch of secretaries and you still couldn't do it. Didn't have the application.
RICHIE. What does he know about it? Lot's of very experienced journalists don't have shorthand. It's not essential. It's very useful but not essential. *(Pause.)* I was a hack ... big deal ... I was hot for a while and now I'm not. *(Pause.)* I'm not a bad typist.
RACHEL. ... Nor am I.
RICHIE. Really? What do you write?
RACHEL. It's not that kind of typing. And I don't suppose it's essential. But it's very useful. *(Long pause.)*
RICHIE. Have you got a typewriter?
RACHEL. I've got a very nice typewriter.
RICHIE. A very nice typewriter? Well that's very nice isn't it? What sort is it?
RACHEL. It's electric. Absolutely electric. Sensitive to the gentlest, most delicate touch. It's outrageous. I mean, when I'm hot, the results are glorious. *(Pause.)*
RICHIE. Are you fast?
RACHEL. Oh, will you stop asking stupid questions? *(Silence.)* I've never felt so guilty in my life.
RICHIE. Have you cheated on him before?
RACHEL. Of course not.
RICHIE. Has he cheated on you?
RACHEL. No.
RICHIE. I never cheated on Nicky.
RACHEL. I'm impressed. *(Pause.)*
RICHIE. I yearn for her. I yearn for her so much I feel ill. Everything aches. Nothing works properly. There isn't a moment I don't think about her.
RACHEL. Really?
RICHIE. Really.
RACHEL. I see. Well ... *(Pause.)* That's me told.

RICHIE. It was just a fuck.
RACHEL. I know it was just a fuck but ...
RICHIE. I mean it wasn't the fuck of the century, it wasn't the shag of a lifetime, I admit ...
RACHEL. It wasn't just a fuck. Not really, was it?
RICHIE. It wasn't even a fuck. I mean strictly speaking Rachel ...
RACHEL. You've made your point. *(Silence. Rachel gets out of bed and dresses.)*
RICHIE. What have I done now?
RACHEL. It's not funny.
RICHIE. Sorry?
RACHEL. It's not funny anymore.
RICHIE. I think it's hysterical.
RACHEL. I know.
RICHIE. I mean ... you have to laugh ...
RACHEL. Do you? Why? *(Pause.)*
RICHIE. I'm not laughing at you.
RACHEL. Aren't you?
RICHIE. I'm laughing with you.
RACHEL. I'm not laughing. *(Pause.)*
RICHIE. You have to laugh, though ...
RACHEL. Why are you doing this? What is wrong with you? Why are you like this? *(Pause.)*
RICHIE. I'm lonely. *(Richie dresses.)*
RACHEL. You're a very strange person, Richie.
RICHIE. I know. *(Silence. Rachel sits on the bed.)*
RACHEL. Tell me what you're thinking.
RICHIE. What do you think I'm thinking?
RACHEL. I don't know Richie. Nobody knows ...
RICHIE. "Fuck" is what I'm thinking. *(Pause.)*
RACHEL. You'll find somebody. One day. You just have to be ... extremely patient. *(Pause.)* I am fond of you. But you're like a lightning rod. You're just too much sometimes.
RICHIE. Sometimes ... *(She gives him a hug. Neal is standing in the doorway. Richie sees him and stares.)*
RICHIE. This isn't what it looks like. *(Pause.)*
NEAL. Why aren't you at work?

RACHEL. I took the day off.
NEAL. Another day off? Dear oh dear. I thought you might have. In fact I had an instinct. I had a sixth sense. *(Pause.)* We must be psychic. It must be because we're so close. *(Pause.)* Anyway. I thought I'd surprise you.
RACHEL. You did.
NEAL. Yes, it seems like I did.
RACHEL. Why aren't you at work?
NEAL. I've resigned. Unexpected isn't it? Are you shocked?
RACHEL. Just a little.
NEAL. That I'm home or that I've resigned?
RACHEL. Why did you resign?
NEAL. Why not? Everybody's doing it. It's a culture of resignation. Go with the flow, I say.
RACHEL. Why?
NEAL. Because I'm not cut out for it. Because I didn't want to lose any more patients. Because I didn't want to lose you. *(Pause.)*
RICHIE. We've been talking.
NEAL. Yes. I thought you might have been. I envy you the opportunity. The thing is, the only thing that puzzles me is, why in here? Why are you in my bedroom again? *(Pause.)* You know what I think? I think you've overstepped the mark a bit. I think you take liberties. I think this time around you've really taken a liberty, coming into my bedroom. And it is my bedroom now.
RACHEL. Neal ...
NEAL. Well he does. You do. You really ... *(Pause.)* You've really shot yourself in the foot this time. You've blown it clean it off. Nobody can help you now. It's gone. Woosh!
RICHIE. You're pissed.
NEAL. I've been drinking, it's true. In the pub. Under a table. Lovely. Sharpening my diagnostic skills. I see everything much clearer when I'm piss-drunk. And my diagnosis is: You're a terminal case. It's irreversible. You could always ask her for a second opinion. She's obviously a little more boned up on the subject ...
RACHEL. That's enough ...

NEAL.   She's put in a bit of overtime on that one. *(Silence.)* Get out. Not you. Him. *(Richie goes.)* Am I imagining this? Tell me it's just my anxiety. Please ...
RACHEL.   Neal ...
NEAL.   Was it good?
RACHEL.   It wasn't anything.
NEAL.   Was it a laugh? Did you laugh? Did you giggle? Did you scream? Did you gasp and say "fuck" at the point of no return? Did you cry out his name as he held you down? Did you kiss his eyes and whisper to him? Did you see something in his eyes? Did he see something in yours? *(Silence.)* Why?

Scene 3

Bar. Night. Richie drinking shots.

RICHIE.   *(Drunk.)* A horse walks into a bar and orders a beer. And the barman says ... Why are you looking so fucking miserable for? Eh? *(He laughs.)* I'm the grandson of a preacherman. The son of a son of a preacherman. No ... hold on ... My mother's father was an Anglican vicar. Never was there a kinder, more sensitive man. Had a love of sheepdogs and wrote stories for *Children's Hour* during the war. My father's father, on the other hand, was an impotent sadistic cocksucker who beat his sons every day with a strap in an attempt to toughen them up for the army. They term "character flaw" springs to mind. *(He drinks a shot.)* This complex and enigmatic combination of sensitivity and viciousness was handed down through generations of emotional fucking cripples, doing for their relationships and later doing for mine. *(He drinks a shot.)* Look at you ... with your smug, bemused grin ... I hope you're sufficiently entertained. I hope you're enjoying this. I drink to and for your delectation ... *(He raises a glass, toasts and drinks.)* You disgust me. What do you know about anything? My problem is that I know too much. I'm too intelligent for this world. And what's more it's my considered and exquisitely elegant analysis that I'm just too fucking sensitive ... *(To the bar in general.)* You're all a bunch of shits ... *(He drinks a shot.)* Are you listening to me? Listen to me ... listen to me ...

Scene 4

Hospital. Richie lying in a bed unconscious. Tubes coming out of his nose and mouth. Neal and Rachel sitting.

NEAL. Where are you staying?
RACHEL. In a hotel. It's not far. I thought we could meet for a drink sometime.
NEAL. Why? *(Silence.)*
RACHEL. I phoned his mum.
NEAL. Thank you. I couldn't face it.
RACHEL. She said she wasn't surprised. Did you phone his dad?
NEAL. I couldn't face it.
RACHEL. You sound miserable.
NEAL. Actually I'm feeling quite perky.
RACHEL. Perky for you I suppose.
NEAL. Yes. Comparatively perky I suppose. *(Pause.)* What is it about somebody else's misery that diminishes your own?
RACHEL. It's a subconscious competition for pity. With Richie we realise there is no competition.
NEAL. Sometimes he makes me feel quite cheerful about my life.
RACHEL. I miss you. *(Pause.)* Do you miss me? *(Silence.)*
NEAL. It's occurred to me that maybe Richie genuinely tries to be good but he's just no good at it.
RACHEL. He's just lonely.

NEAL.   Lonely? *(Pause.)* I'm lonely. Everybody's lonely.
RACHEL.   Are you?
NEAL.   No ... I'm just saying ...
RACHEL.   What are you saying? *(Pause.)*
NEAL.   Maybe I am too uptight about things. I admit it, I am like an old woman sometimes. *(Richie stirs briefly.)*
RACHEL.   Look. He moved.
NEAL.   He does that from time to time. It doesn't mean anything. *(Pause.)* Do you want to read to him?
RACHEL.   I think he'd prefer it if you read.
NEAL.   I only have Crime.
RACHEL.   It's not important. It's just the aural stimulation that's important.
NEAL.   Yes but Crime Rachel. Do you think that's wise?
RACHEL.   Crime's fine. *(Neal reads.)*
NEAL.   "'We don't have many crooks here in Central City, ma'am,' I said. 'Anyway, people are people, even when they're a little misguided. You don't hurt them, they won't hurt you. They'll listen to reason.' She shook her head, wide-eyed with awe ..." *(Lights down. Lights up. Rachel standing. Neal sitting. Richie unconscious.)*
RACHEL.   I did all the books.
NEAL.   Sorry?
RACHEL.   I separated our books.
NEAL.   Oh. Thank you.
RACHEL.   I sorted yours out for you too. Text books on the bottom, real books on the top. It goes Arthritis to Dermatology, then Endocrinology to Pediatrics ... then cowboy books.
NEAL.   What have you done with my cowboy books?
RACHEL.   They're on the top. With Crime. And I've taken the wok.
NEAL.   You've taken the wok?
RACHEL.   Is that all right?
NEAL.   What did you take the wok for? It's my wok.
RACHEL.   I didn't think you'd use it.
NEAL.   That's not the point. It's mine.
RACHEL.   You've got the big frying pan.
NEAL.   I need the big wok. It's not the same.

RACHEL.   What's the difference?
NEAL.   Well ... if you don't know the difference between a wok and a frying pan then I'm not telling you.
RACHEL.   All right ...
NEAL.   Well there's a principle at stake.
RACHEL.   I gave you that wok for your birthday.
NEAL.   So?
RACHEL.   So ... don't be so mingy.
NEAL.   Mingy?
RACHEL.   Mingy. Yes. You're being mingy and mean-spirited about the whole business.
NEAL.   Well if you say so then I must be.
RACHEL.   Neal ...
NEAL.   I'm mingy. I'm mean-spirited and mingy and jumpy and uptight. Fine. Fine. Who cares? *(Pause.)* I hope you didn't take my shower curtain.
RACHEL.   What?
NEAL.   The shower curtain. I like that shower curtain. It matches the tiles. *(Pause.)* Not the green ones. The other ones. With the pattern. With the little, slightly rococo seashell stencil ...
RACHEL.   Oh I've had enough of this. *(She starts to go.)*
NEAL.   Don't walk away from me when I'm talking to you.
RACHEL.   I thought we could do this together. I thought you might like to help me. I thought if we did this together and we talked about it and we ... talked about a few other things it might be a bit easier. I thought I could come over and we could go through our things and talk about it properly and separate our things and then when this is all over ... when I find somewhere to go ... you could come over for dinner or something. I thought I'd cook you dinner. I thought it would be nice. I thought I was making a gesture. I thought it might help me to say I'm sorry. Because I am sorry. I am ... so sorry Neal ... and I'm trying not to make a scene and I'm trying to be sensitive about this and I'm trying ... not to be so sensitive about this and just get on with it ... I'm trying to be practical ... I'm trying not to get all emotional about it ... that's why I took the stupid fucking wok. *(Silence.)* Nicky phoned for you.
NEAL.   Nicky?

RACHEL. Yesterday. While I was doing the bathroom stuff.
NEAL. Did you find my shaving brush? Only I can't find it. I thought he might have taken it but then I thought that that was just daft. *(Pause.)* Sorry. Go on.
RACHEL. She wanted your address so she could send on some of Richie's things. I told her what's happened and asked her to think about coming home. She said she wouldn't come home even if he were dying.
NEAL. He is dying. *(Rachel produces a scrap of paper and gives it to Neal.)*
RACHEL. She left the number of the hotel where she's staying. Will you give it to him?
NEAL. Do you think she still loves him?
RACHEL. Maybe. Maybe not.
NEAL. Do you think she ever loved him?
RACHEL. I'm sure she adored him once. *(Silence. Richie stirs. He opens his eyes. Books fall to the floor.)*
NEAL. Richie? My God.
RICHIE. Who are you?
NEAL. You don't recognize me?
RICHIE. No. You're some kind of shrink or something.
RACHEL. Richie, look at me.
RICHIE. What the fuck is going on here? *(He looks around.)*
RACHEL. You're in hospital. You've been very poorly. *(He looks at her.)*
RICHIE. Can you get me something to eat? I'm starved.
RACHEL. I'll get the doctor. *(She exits. He looks at Neal.)*
RICHIE. I adore nurses.
NEAL. I thought you weren't going to make it.
RICHIE. Well you're a morbid bastard aren't you?
NEAL. Can't you remember anything? *(Pause.)*
RICHIE. Something about ... the river? *(Pause. He smiles.)* I expect this means I'll never be best man. *(Pause.)* My head is throbbing.
NEAL. Hurts, does it?
RICHIE. It's throbbing.
NEAL. Tell me if this hurts. *(Neal probes Richie's head forcefully.)*
RICHIE. Ow! What did you do that for?

NEAL. And this? *(He does it again.)*
RICHIE. Will you stop doing that? Are you insane? *(Pause.)* You're a fucking doctor. *(Neal slaps and chokes Richie. He stops and they stare at each other. Silence. Lights down.)*

Scene 5

Neal and Rachel's flat. Afternoon. Neal, standing, drinking Scotch, drunk. A large box is in the middle of the floor. Richie sitting, staring at the box. Neal lights a cigarette and offers one to Richie.

NEAL. Want one?
RICHIE. Thanks but I couldn't
NEAL. You haven't smoked in, what is it, a week now?
RICHIE. More or less, yes.
NEAL. Splendid. Or is it two weeks?
RICHIE. I don't remember.
NEAL. Not since your overdose. Very wise. *(Pause.)* I like smoking. I think it's marvelous. I can't imagine what stopped me before. I can't believe I actually refrained from shamelessly indulging myself merely as a matter of principle. *(Neal pours another glass of Scotch and drinks.)*
RICHIE. Thanks for picking me up from the hospital.
NEAL. Nobody else would.
RICHIE. And thanks for visiting me.
NEAL. You'd do the same for me.
RICHIE. I would. Well, of course I would.
NEAL. Of course ...
RICHIE. I'm being sincere Neal.
NEAL. I don't recommend that. It never worked for me.
RICHIE. I've changed. I feel almost absurdly positive about everything now. It's quite incredible. *(Pause.)* While I was in a hospital I had an epiphany.

NEAL. An epiphany, eh?
RICHIE. It was like I went outside of my body.
NEAL. An out of body experience?
RICHIE. Absolutely.
NEAL. Happens all the time.
RICHIE. It was more than that.
NEAL. It's all to do with the brain.
RICHIE. I floated above my body and I looked down and I saw myself lying there, and I saw people gathered around, being very concerned, and ... I felt very strange. I felt like I wanted to cry. I mean, it wasn't the fact that I was in hospital. It was the fact that other people were concerned about me. It was ... the concern that got to me. *(Pause.)*
NEAL. Ridiculous ...
RICHIE. It really surprised me.
NEAL. It surprises me. Who on earth were these people?
RICHIE. Well, you, presumably. And Rachel.
NEAL. I see.
RICHIE. I mean, really, it really meant something.
NEAL. Really?
RICHIE. Yes. And I thought about you and your life. I mean really thought about it, and it occurred to me that whatever I've seen in my life, however terrible or ... pathetic, you've seen worse.
NEAL. What have you seen?
RICHIE. Eh?
NEAL. What have you seen that's so terrible? You're an old drama Queen.
RICHIE. Precisely. What have I seen? You've seen the insides of a human being. Got right in there to the ugly, bloody, stinking core and you still smell like a biscuit factory. Still get up in the morning and shave and do the job. At least you did until I got here. *(Pause.)* And there and then, I resolved to be a good, honest man. Redeem my entire sorry life. Settle down. Give up drinking. Work even.
NEAL. Work? I wouldn't recommend that.
RICHIE. Why not?
NEAL. You'll get screwed.

RICHIE. Why should I get screwed?
NEAL. Look at me.
RICHIE. I agree, but ...
NEAL. You agree that you'd get screwed or you agree that I've been screwed?
RICHIE. I ... both ...
NEAL. Rachel's probably being screwed right at this very minute. Which is her prerogative. But you see I think you've screwed yourself.
RICHIE. Don't take the piss.
NEAL. On the contrary. I will take the piss. I think I have every right to take the piss. Because if you think about it Richie, it's probably my turn to take the piss now. *(Pause.)*
RICHIE. You know what your problem is? You've become cynical.
NEAL. You know what kind of people call other people cynics?
RICHIE. What?
NEAL. Idiots. Cynics are realists ... surrounded by idiots.
RICHIE. I'm trying to say I'm sorry.
NEAL. "Sorry." Mm. You know, I'm not sure I actually really know what that word means. And I'm fucking certain that you don't. *(Long pause.)*
RICHIE. Well ... I'll be off then.
NEAL. Are you really going to Wales?
RICHIE. Yes.
NEAL. What are you going to do?
RICHIE. I'm going to buy a little cottage and bury myself in life-affirming toil. What the fuck do you think I'm going to do?
NEAL. And wait for Nicky? Did I tell you she rang? *(Pause.)*
RICHIE. No. You didn't.
NEAL. She told Rachel that she wouldn't come home even if you were on your deathbed. The funny thing was, at the time, you were on your deathbed.
RICHIE. When was this?
NEAL. When you were on your deathbed.
RICHIE. Did she leave a message? A phone number?
NEAL. No. Well, you could ask Rachel, only I don't have a number for her either.

RICHIE. Well, where is she?
NEAL. I don't know. Who cares?
RICHIE. "Who cares?"
NEAL. Who cares? *(Neal drinks. Richie goes to the box and opens it hesitantly. He produces a sombrero and puts it on. He produces a letter, opens it, reads).*
RICHIE. She's sent all my things. She sent some of hers too. It isn't because she's joining me, she says it's because she can't bear to be reminded of the time we spent together. It think it's a good sign. *(He produces a poncho, sniffs it.)* I can still smell her perfume. Look ... one of her hairs. *(He takes off lint and a stray hair. He puts the poncho on. Pause. He blows his nose on the poncho. He takes the bottle from Neal. Drinks.)*
NEAL. Have you bought your ticket yet?
RICHIE. Not yet.
NEAL. Do you know how much a ticket to Wales is?
RICHIE. No idea.
NEAL. Have you got any money?
RICHIE. A little ...
NEAL. Have you got anywhere to stay?
RICHIE. I thought I'd just busk it.
NEAL. Do you know anybody in Wales?
RICHIE. You know I don't.
NEAL. Not a soul? Ah. *(Neal takes out his wallet, offers money.)*
RICHIE. I couldn't. It's time I stood on my own two feet again.
NEAL. Take it. *(Richie finds his suitcase and packs clothes from the box into the case.)*
RICHIE. I've taken enough from you.
NEAL. Oh I know that. No, I'm not denying that. But I want you out of my hair.
RICHIE. If you insist. *(Richie takes the money.)* I'm going to miss you. *(Pause. He packs.)*
NEAL. I'll come with you. Make sure you get your train.
RICHIE. I said I'll miss you. *(He shuts his case and stands holding it.)* I'll probably be back in a year or two. You know me. You don't get rid of me that easily.
NEAL. I tell you what. I'll call you a cab. It's pissing down.
RICHIE. Thanks. Thanks for everything. You're a real friend.

(He goes to embrace Neal. Neal turns away, picks up the phone and dials.)

Scene 6

Pub. Evening. Rachel is sitting at a garden table, smoking. Neal approaches the table with drinks. A pint for him. A vodka and orange for her. He sits.

RACHEL. I've got a new flat. Well, it's just a bedsit really. New Cross.
NEAL. New Cross? Nice.
RACHEL. It's near the practice. Sometimes I wander into Goldsmith's for a cup of coffee. It's nice to just sit there amongst the students. Look at all the noticeboards. There's always something going on.
NEAL. You're looking well.
RACHEL. So are you.
NEAL. Are you? Are you well? *(Rachel yawns.)*
RACHEL. I'm tired.
NEAL. Are you really? I couldn't tell. What have you been doing?
RACHEL. Just sleeping.
NEAL. Well what have you been doing to make you sleep.
RACHEL. I went out last night with ... *(She yawns.)*
NEAL. Who? With who? *(She yawns.)*
RACHEL. Just a friend. One of the partners.
NEAL. You look terrible.
RACHEL. Thank you.
NEAL. Well, you know ...
RACHEL. I know. You worry. *(They sip their drinks. She yawns.)* I've just been working too hard.
NEAL. It's time you did what you want to do.
RACHEL. I want to make money.

NEAL.   They treat you like a slave.
RACHEL.   I know.
NEAL.   Well do something about it. You've always wanted to change your life. Now's your chance. *(Pause.)*
RACHEL.   Do you still think you made the right decision?
NEAL.   Absolutely. I think so. I'm almost sure I did and if I didn't ...
RICHIE.   I meant us. *(Pause.)*
NEAL.   I don't know what I think. I won't know for a while.
RACHEL.   When will you know?
NEAL.   Months probably. Anyway. I like it like this. I think about it a lot. I worry I made the wrong decision and that one day I'll wake up and realise and it'll be too late ... I do ... but I also like this. I like meeting you now just for a drink by the river. For the first time in my life I feel free. Do you realise that? I've never been free. I've never been single and unemployed before. These are exciting times for me. *(Pause.)*
RACHEL.   We've had drinks by the river before.
NEAL.   Have we? I don't think so.
RACHEL.   When we lived in Kilburn.
NEAL.   That wasn't by the river, it was by the canal.
RACHEL.   Well, anyway ...
NEAL.   There is a difference. *(Silence.)*
RACHEL.   I was thinking of going away for the bank holiday. I've got some time off. Come with me if you like.
NEAL.   Where do you want to go?
RACHEL.   Anywhere. Who cares? *(Pause.)*
NEAL.   Have you thought about going abroad?
RACHEL.   Oh. I can't be bothered.
NEAL.   Not for the weekend. For a while. See the world. Do what you've always wanted to.
RACHEL.   I can't be bothered. No ... Not anymore. *(Pause.)* I'd be lonely.
NEAL.   You know what your problem is?
RACHEL.   What?
NEAL.   You're a hopeless romantic.
RACHEL.   What's wrong with that?
NEAL.   It's hopeless. *(Silence.)*

RACHEL. Do you think we made a good couple?
NEAL. You know I do.
RACHEL. But it was more than that wasn't it?
NEAL. In what respect?
RACHEL. We were more than just "a couple," weren't we? It was more than that, wasn't it?
NEAL. I suppose it was.
RACHEL. We were such good friends. Such good friends.
NEAL. Absolutely.
RACHEL. Soul-mates.
NEAL. Good lovers. I mean ...
RACHEL. Kindred spirits.
NEAL. And good lovers. Comparatively ...
RACHEL. And good lovers. Absolutely. *(Silence.)*
NEAL. Richie and I were good friends once. I learnt a lot from him.
RACHEL. What did you learn?
NEAL. I learnt what it's like to want to kill somebody. The things is, I always expected him to change. I never expected you to change. And then you did and he didn't. *(Pause.)*
RACHEL. Did I?
NEAL. I don't know. But I'm saying I didn't expect ...
RACHEL. What did you expect? What did you want from me in all those years? Marriage? Stability? Children?
NEAL. I wanted you, I just wanted ... you. *(Pause. He drinks. The stage slowly darkens as twilight sets in.)* I had a dream about you last night. We were on a roof and it was very dark, night time, brilliant stars in the sky. It was a roof party. A barbecue on a midsummer night. And you could see right across London, all the places we'd lived together. The river and the Embankment and the water glittering in the dark. And I wasn't really talking to you but you came over in a black dress and started talking to me. You were laughing insistently at something or other and I started laughing, humouring you, in my dream, and then I saw it. This thing on your breast, like a broach, over your heart. A cluster. As I got closer I saw it was a nest of maggots. And as we were laughing the maggots grew and hatched more maggots. And I thought of Richie. And that's when I finally knew it was over. I

would never be in love with you again. We'd walk away from each other quite calmly and you'd never even notice you had this thing clinging to you. Nobody would. Only I would. *(Pause.)* And then I realised it wasn't maggots at all. It was rice pudding. Or bubble and squeak. That's what you'd been laughing about. Bubble and squeak all down your dress. And I went to kiss you. And I woke up. *(Pause.)* What do you think it means. *(Pause.)*
RACHEL.   Do you want another drink? *(Silence. Blackout.)*

PROPERTY LIST

Pint of milk (RICHIE)
Suitcase (RICHIE)
Coffee pot and coffee (NEAL)
Cigarettes and matches (RICHIE, NEAL, RACHEL)
Ashtray (NEAL)
Bottle of Scotch (RICHIE, NEAL)
Blanket and pillow (NEAL)
Scans (NEAL)
Gray's Anatomy (NEAL)
Vial (RICHIE)
Wallet with tenner (NEAL)
Drinks (RICHIE, RACHEL, NEAL)
Vial and syringe (NEAL)
Ketamine (RICHIE)
Money (NEAL)
Kettle (RACHEL)
Cornflowers (RACHEL)
Wine bottle with glasses (NEAL, RACHEL, RICHIE)
Shot glasses (RICHIE)
Scrap of paper (RACHEL)
Books (RICHIE)
Box (RICHIE) with:
    sombrero
    letter
    poncho

SOUND EFFECTS

Plane

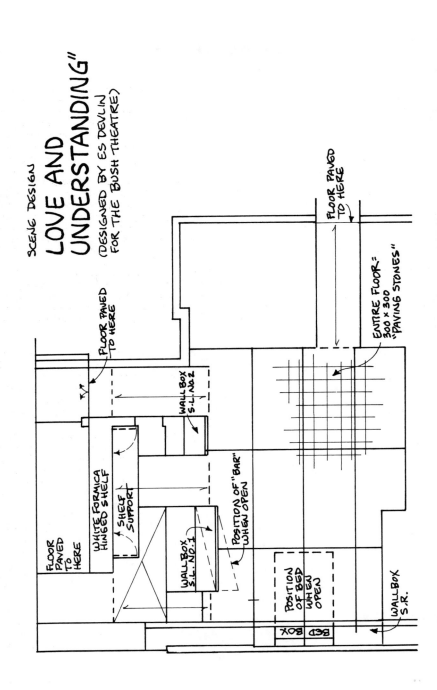

NEW PLAYS

- **SMASH by Jeffrey Hatcher.** Based on the novel, AN UNSOCIAL SOCIALIST by George Bernard Shaw, the story centers on a millionaire Socialist who leaves his bride on their wedding day because he fears his passion for her will get in the way of his plans to overthrow the British government. *"SMASH is witty, cunning, intelligent, and skillful."* –Seattle Weekly. *"SMASH is a wonderfully high-style British comedy of manners that evokes the world of Shaw's high-minded heroes and heroines, but shaped by a post modern sensibility."* –Seattle Herald. [5M, 5W] ISBN: 0-8222-1553-5

- **PRIVATE EYES by Steven Dietz.** A comedy of suspicion in which nothing is ever quite what it seems. *"Steven Dietz's ... Pirandellian smooch to the mercurial nature of theatrical illusion and romantic truth, Dietz's spiraling structure and breathless pacing provide enough of an oxygen rush to revive any moribund audience member ... Dietz's mastery of playmaking ... is cause for kudos."* –The Village Voice. *"The cleverest and most artful piece presented at the 21st annual [Humana] festival was PRIVATE EYES by writer-director Steven Dietz."* –The Chicago Tribune. [3M, 2W] ISBN: 0-8222-1619-1

- **DIMLY PERCEIVED THREATS TO THE SYSTEM by Jon Klein.** Reality and fantasy overlap with hilarious results as this unforgettable family attempts to survive the nineties. *"Here's a play whose point about fractured families goes to the heart, mind -- and ears."* –The Washington Post. *" ... an end-of-the millennium comedy about a family on the verge of a nervous breakdown ... Trenchant and hilarious ... "* –The Baltimore Sun. [2M, 4W] ISBN: 0-8222-1677-9

- **HONOUR by Joanna Murray-Smith.** In a series of intense confrontations, a wife, husband, lover and daughter negotiate the forces of passion, lust, history, responsibility and honour. *"Tight, crackling dialogue (usually played out in punchy verbal duels) captures characters unable to deal with emotions ... Murray-Smith effectively places her characters in situations that strip away pretense."* –Variety. *"HONOUR might just capture a few honors of its own."* –Time Out Magazine. [1M, 3W] ISBN: 0-8222-1683-3

- **NINE ARMENIANS by Leslie Ayvazian.** A revealing portrait of three generations of an Armenian-American family. *" ... Ayvazian's obvious personal exploration ... is evocative, and her picture of an American Life colored nostalgically by an increasingly alien ethnic tradition, is persuasively embedded into a script of a certain supple grace ... "* –The NY Post. *"... NINE ARMENIANS is a warm, likable work that benefits from ... Ayvazian's clear-headed insight into the dynamics of a close-knit family ... "* –Variety. [5M, 5W] ISBN: 0-8222-1602-7

- **PSYCHOPATHIA SEXUALIS by John Patrick Shanley.** Fetishes and psychiatry abound in this scathing comedy about a man and his father's argyle socks. *"John Patrick Shanley's new play, PSYCHOPATHIA SEXUALIS is ... perfectly poised between daffy comedy and believable human neurosis which Shanley combines so well ... "* –The LA Times. *"John Patrick Shanley's PSYCHOPATHIA SEXUALIS is a salty boulevard comedy with a bittersweet theme ... "* –New York Magazine. *"A tour de force of witty, barbed dialogue."* –Variety. [3M, 2W] ISBN: 0-8222-1615-9

DRAMATISTS PLAY SERVICE, INC.
440 Park Avenue South, New York, NY 10016 212-683-8960 Fax 212-213-1539
postmaster@dramatists.com www.dramatists.com

NEW PLAYS

- **A QUESTION OF MERCY** by David Rabe. The Obie Award-winning playwright probes the sensitive and controversial issue of doctor-assisted suicide in the age of AIDS in this poignant drama. *"There are many devastating ironies in Mr. Rabe's beautifully considered, piercingly clear-eyed work ... " —The NY Times.* "With unsettling candor and disturbing insight, the play arouses pity and understanding of a troubling subject ... Rabe's provocative tale is an affirmation of dignity that rings clear and true." —Variety. [6M, 1W] ISBN: 0-8222-1643-4

- **A DOLL'S HOUSE** by Henrik Ibsen, adapted by Frank McGuinness. Winner of the 1997 Tony Award for best revival. "New, raw, gut-twisting and gripping. Easily the hottest drama this season." —USA Today. "Bold, brilliant and alive." —The Wall Street Journal. "A thunderclap of an evening that takes your breath away." —Time. "The stuff of Broadway legend." —Associated Press. [4M, 4W, 2 boys] ISBN: 0-8222-1636-1

- **THE WAITING ROOM** by Lisa Loomer. Three women from different centuries meet in a doctor's waiting room in this dark comedy about the timeless quest for beauty -- and its cost. "... THE WAITING ROOM ... is a bold, risky melange of conflicting elements that is ... terrifically moving ... There's no resisting the fierce emotional pull of the play." —The NY Times. " ... one of the high points of this year's Off-Broadway season ... THE WAITING ROOM is well worth a visit." —Back Stage. [7M, 4W, flexible casting] ISBN: 0-8222-1594-2

- **MR. PETERS' CONNECTIONS** by Arthur Miller. Mr. Miller describes the protagonist as existing in a dream-like state when the mind is "freed to roam from real memories to conjectures, from trivialities to tragic insights, from terror of death to glorying in one's being alive." With this memory play, the Tony Award and Pulitzer Prize-winner reaffirms his stature as the world's foremost dramatist. " ... *a cross between Joycean stream-of-consciousness and Strindberg's dream plays, sweetened with a dose of William Saroyan's philosophical whimsy ... CONNECTIONS is most intriguing ... Miller scholars will surely find many connections of their own to make between this work and the author's earlier plays." —The NY Times.* [5M, 3W] ISBN: 0-8222-1687-6

- **THE STEWARD OF CHRISTENDOM** by Sebastian Barry. A freely imagined portrait of the author's great-grandfather, the last Chief Superintendent of the Dublin Metropolitan Police. "MAGNIFICENT ... the cool, elegiac eye of James Joyce's THE DEAD; the bleak absurdity of Samuel Beckett's lost, primal characters; the cosmic anger of KING LEAR ..." —The NY Times. "Sebastian Barry's compassionate imaging of an ancestor he never knew is among the most poignant onstage displays of humanity in recent memory." —Variety. [5M, 4W] ISBN: 0-8222-1609-4

- **SYMPATHETIC MAGIC** by Lanford Wilson. Winner of the 1997 Obie for best play. The mysteries of the universe, and of human and artistic creation, are explored in this award-winning play. "Lanford Wilson's idiosyncratic SYMPATHETIC MAGIC is his BEST PLAY YET ... the rare play you WANT ... chock-full of ideas, incidents, witty or poetic lines, scientific and philosophical argument ... you'll find your intellectual faculties racing." —New York Magazine. "The script is like a fully notated score, next to which most new plays are cursory lead sheets." —The Village Voice. [5M, 3W] ISBN: 0-8222-1630-2

DRAMATISTS PLAY SERVICE, INC.
440 Park Avenue South, New York, NY 10016 212-683-8960 Fax 212-213-1539
postmaster@dramatists.com www.dramatists.com